The Well-Managed Ministry

The Well-Managed Ministry

VICTOR BOOKS®

A DIVISION OF SCRIPTURE PRESS PUBLICATIONS INC.
USA CANADA ENGLAND

Scripture quotations are from *New American Standard Bible,* © the Lockman Foundation 1960, 1962, 1963, 1968, 1971, 1972, 1973, 1975, 1977.

Recommended Dewey Decimal Classification: 267.33
Suggested Subject Heading: ASSOCIATIONS FOR RELIGIOUS WORK: ORGANIZATION AND
ADMINISTRATION

Library of Congress Catalog Number: 89-060174
ISBN: 0-89693-736-4

CONTENTS

PREFACE

Christian organizations have a unique mission, and thus require some distinctive approaches in their management. Though modern management theory is transferable in a variety of ways from one type of organization to another, it is definitely not value neutral. Management techniques are laden with philosophical implications, many of which may stand in tension with Christian values.

The setting in which management is practiced largely determines the values which underlie management techniques. Certain managerial approaches that are appropriate for today's business world are inappropriate for Christian organizations, which have some distinctly different components to their mission. In the light of this tension, a primary purpose of this resource handbook is to help Christian professionals develop a personal management style compatible with their values.

Too often Christian professionals feel inadequate as administrators because of limited management education and misconceptions about the nature and complexity of administration. Indeed management can become difficult at times, but this is often the result of the manager's professional deficiencies and shortcomings. When practiced competently, management is not an enormously difficult undertaking. A second purpose of this handbook is to assist the busy, often burdened, Christian professional in developing a style of management that works efficiently and effectively. While this handbook does not promise to make management "easy," its resources are designed to help Christian workers contend successfully with the administrative challenges that inevitably are part of their organizational role.

This book is written in a "modular" format designed to make management practical, easy-to-digest, and action-oriented—in short, "user-friendly." Though not a "cookbook" promising simplistic answers to complex questions, the book does strive to provide pragmatic action guidelines for both administrative thinking and action. The format of content modules and worksheets is expressly designed to focus the reader on only the most essential management skills and realities—those that typically have the greatest influence on achieving results. In every toolbox certain tools receive more frequent use; this handbook is constructed from the "pliers, screwdrivers, and wrenches" of managing in a Christian setting.

The book is designed to promote interactive group discussion and exchange. Team members can sit down together and engage in productive dialogue about ministry productivity, progress, and potential.

Team leaders are provided with a practical resource for tackling complex managerial problems that require a team solution.

Each of the ten chapters explores a key component of effective management. The reader is provided with both descriptive and prescriptive insights into chapter topics through three format features: *Discussion Modules, Situation Reviews, and Action Plans.* These provide a meaningful structure for organizational insight, problem diagnosis, identification and evaluation of action alternatives, goal-setting, and implementation.

The series of practical Discussion Modules provide sharp, focused insight into the true nature of managing in a Christian setting. This content material is up-to-date, easy to absorb, and combines both descriptive and prescriptive perspectives. The Situation Reviews, which focus on the past and present, help ministry team members better understand their personal management styles and what makes their ministries "tick." The future-focused Action Plans facilitate practical planning for the future, highlighting ways in which ministry effectiveness can be further enhanced.

A biblical perspective on management is presented throughout the workbook. The following ten seminal themes are reflected directly and indirectly in the discussion material:

1. The purpose of management in Christian organizations is to create a fertile climate for spiritual service—a sense of shared mission, wise stewardship of resources, and mutual supportiveness.

2. The purpose of a Christian ministry is not excellent management per se. Management is merely a means to the end of serving God.

3. Ministry team members are valued not only for their performance contributions to the ministry, but also because they are members of God's family.

4. The ministry team is to be a "family" of people who care about and for one another.

5. Management of Christian organizations is to be people-centered and participative.

6. Ministry management places a high value on cooperation and teamwork.

8

7. Team members are motivated by a shared sense of vision and mission, which is more important to them than personal gain. Goals are pursued selflessly and sacrificially.

8. How Christians work with one another is just as important as what they are striving to accomplish.

9. A key aim of ministry management is to help team members become more Christlike.

10. Management in Christian organizations is ultimately a partnership with God, built on prayer, faith, and obedience.

The ministry leader/manager faces three central challenges in using this resource book. First, *a team approach must be maintained,* calling for an open mind, patience, and the willingness to do things other people's way. The second challenge is to *avoid emulating the world's management model,* with its all-too-familiar emphasis on economic goals, pressure to perform, rugged individualism, and self-serving competitiveness. The third, and most difficult challenge, is to *accept human imperfection*—to live with one another's mistakes, shortcomings, and foibles. In the final analysis, love is the sole foundation of management in Christian organizations. "By this all men will know that you are My disciples, if you have love for one another" (John 13:35).

INTRODUCTION:

USING THIS BOOK TO BUILD
TEAMWORK IN YOUR MINISTRY

The Well-Managed Ministry is a multifaceted and professional resource that can be beneficially used by individuals and by teams. Its materials are carefully designed to stimulate ministry excellence and productivity. The book promotes both the *understanding* and the *practice* of effective management within a Christian setting.

Discussion Modules strategically interspersed throughout the chapters present insight into the essential functions, skills, and activities of management. These focused, fast-flowing modules of information provide a basic introduction to the ends and means of Christian management for ministerial staff and lay leaders alike. They can be studied individually by the busy person who wants to get "up-to-speed" in management, or collectively by several people who want to pool their experience.

The Situation Review accompanying each Discussion Module helps team members to *describe* the ministry's status quo. Where are we? Where have we been? Where do we as a team want to go? Through the series of interwoven questionnaires and other self-revealing worksheets, team members are able to assess ministry progress and areas of needed improvement in an objective, interactive fashion. The Situation Reviews are engineered to provoke, challenge, clarify, and measure, enabling team members to get a handle on managing the collective ministry effort in a creative way.

Following each Situation Review is a future-focused Action Plan designed to put "wheels" on ministry plans and aspirations—a *prescriptive* perspective. Team members put their heads together to anticipate the future. How can we overcome the status quo? Where can we improve? When is the right time to initiate change? What is each person's most productive role on the team? These concrete Action Plans enable the leader and teammates to work on one practical step at a time—to work smarter in addition to harder.

Team effectiveness is undergirded by several foundational principles. These should stay on the "front burner" of the team leader's mind at all times as the book is used:

1. People need one another, derive identity from one another, and benefit from working together. Teamwork isn't a luxury; it's a necessity!

11

2. Managers must not only do the right things, they must do things in the right way. *How* people work together is extremely significant in Christian ministry.
3. Training and equipping others to perform for the team yields far more ministry fruit over the long run than efforts by the team leader to work harder and longer. Delegation pays irreplaceable dividends.
4. Unilateral decisions are quick to make but slow to implement. Decisions derived from team participation and consensus take longer to make but are backed up by greater cooperation and commitment.
5. Most creative ideas are "hatched" in a group environment as the result of spontaneous brainstorming and freedom from bureaucratic constraints (chain of command, rules, paperwork, etc.). Isolation and routine are poor incubators of creativity.
6. People can work well together even when they have differences of opinion. They can "agree to disagree agreeably."
7. Individual accountability is a catalyst for team productivity.
8. Open, loving confrontation is always preferable to hidden agendas and bottled up frustrations.
9. Forgiveness is the oil and grease of interpersonal relations.
10. Teams need good followers just as much as they need good leaders.

A GAMEPLAN FOR USING THE BOOK

Since the book is designed expressly for interactive hands-on use, members of the ministry team should have a personal copy. This will encourage them to "spread their scent" all over the book by underlining, writing notes in the margins, and so forth. A show and tell atmosphere of comparing personal perspectives will undoubtedly stimulate spontaneous conversation about ministry management needs. The book in and of itself won't provide answers to these issues, but it will definitely prove to be a *catalyst* for the team to generate its own tailor-made solutions.

An excellent way to start using the book is to have team members individually overview its basic contents, highlighting the discussion material and worksheet activities they find most relevant. These can then be given the highest priority for subsequent group discussions and meetings.

Once team members have crystallized how they can put the book to best use, periodic discussion/brainstorming sessions should be scheduled. Such advance planning will help insure not only that the resource materials are actually used, but that each team member is well pre-pared for the fluid, free-floating discussion sessions that will ensue. Who exactly should be included in these meetings? A simple rule of thumb is to include everyone in the organization who is *directly* influ-enced by the ministry—at least for those team meetings of greatest personal relevance.

The team leader should coordinate the periodic team get-togethers, making certain that the purpose and process of each session are clear-ly spelled out to facilitate individual homework. Team members should know in advance which pages of the book are to be read and filled out. If an extended retreat format is to be used, the coordinator would be wise to prepare a time-phased meeting agenda to keep things from bogging down.

During brainstorming sessions, team members can use the book's questions to generate additional probing queries. The team leader, however, must patiently strive to bring about discussion closure, help-ing members forge a productive consensus. Differences of opinions provide an opportunity for team members to get to know one another better. Where consensus cannot be reached, goals should be set for working toward this eventuality in future team sessions.

As teammates work their way through the book's various scored questionnaires, they should bear in mind that these too are designed only to stimulate thinking and brainstorming. They're not validated scientific instruments yielding right and wrong answers on the issues. The questionnaires are but another resource to stimulate insightful analysis.

Different people and teams will use the book in different ways. That's the way it's designed—to be a general purpose resource book serving both individuals and groups in a variety of ways. The more people use the book's resources *together,* the more gold they can mine from it! "Without consultation, plans are frustrated, but with many counselors they succeed" (Proverbs 15:22).

MEDITATIONS FOR
PERSONAL PRODUCTIVITY

Fight the good fight of faith; take hold of the eternal life to which you were called, and you made the good confession in the presence of many witnesses (1 Timothy 6:12).

Suffer hardship with me, as a good soldier of Christ Jesus (2 Timothy 2:3).

And whoever in the name of a disciple gives to one of these little ones even a cup of cold water to drink, truly I say to you he shall not lose his reward (Matthew 10:42).

Come to Me, all who are weary and heavy-laden, and I will give you rest. Take my yoke upon you, and learn from Me, for I am gentle and humble in heart; and you shall find rest for your souls. For My yoke is easy, and My load is light (Matthew 11:28-30).

Therefore if any man is in Christ, he is a new creature; the old things passed away; behold, new things have come (2 Corinthians 5:17).

Chapter 1

Resources for Personal Productivity

■ DISCUSSION MODULE 1.1
EFFECTIVENESS AND EFFICIENCY

In all organizations, achieving results is what counts—but what results? Managers must be concerned not only with "making things happen," but also with how they happen. Both ends (organization goals) and means (management processes) are relevant in the discussion of how to achieve results. Management effectiveness concerns what is accomplished.

Christian ministry professionals should think of effectiveness and efficiency as opposite sides of the same coin, so complementary are they. *How* something is accomplished in ministry is as much an end as *what* is accomplished. Christians should be distinguished not only by the kinds of goals they pursue, but also by how they treat one another while in pursuit.

In secular organizations, efficiency (how people achieve goals) is typically defined along economic lines—time, energy, and dollars saved—rather than along human lines—how people feel about their work and how the organization supports them as they work. Achieving results ordinarily takes precedence over how results are accomplished.

Christian organizations must not define efficiency only in this narrow economic sense. How people feel about achieving results is of great significance, because Christian organizations have human welfare goals as well. The ministry manager should strive to maintain a healthy balance between effectiveness and efficiency. Christian goals must not be achieved at the expense of people. Workaholism, severe pressure to perform, and hard-nosed competitiveness have no place in a ministry setting.

The following Situation Review is designed to help the ministry manager maintain a healthy balance between effectiveness and efficiency.

▲ SITUATION REVIEW 1.1
BALANCING EFFECTIVENESS AND EFFICIENCY

1. To what extent do the people in your organization and specific ministry area feel driven to achieve goals?

_____

_____

_____

_____

_____

2. In the past, how did your organization react when goals were not met? How did you react?

_____

_____

_____

_____

_____

3. In what ways do you feel most constrained and limited in pursuing ministry goals?

_____

_____

_____

_____

_____

4. How do these constraints affect the way you interact with the members of your ministry team?

_____

_____

_____

_____

_____

5. What have you accomplished with the people in your ministry apart from any goals reached (e.g., rapport-building, sense of mutual supportiveness)?

_____

_____

_____

_____

_____

6. To what extent do you have a clear sense of how you want to interrelate with the members of your ministry team?

_____

_____

_____

_____

_____

● ACTION PLAN 1.1
BALANCING EFFECTIVENESS AND EFFICIENCY

1. For each of the major goals your ministry is currently pursuing, list one or two ways you can supportively interact with team members (even if these goals are never satisfactorily achieved):

Ministry goal 1: _____

_____

Means of supportive interaction: _____

_____

_____

_____

Ministry goal 2: _____

_____

Means of supportive interaction: _____

_____

_____

_____

Ministry goal 3: _____

_____

Means of supportive interaction: _____

_____

_____

_____

2. In what ways do you most commonly interact with other members of your organization? Develop several concrete goals for improving the quality of these interactions:

Interaction goal 1: _____

_____

Interaction goal 2: _____

_____

Interaction goal 3: _____

_____

Interaction goal 4: _____

_____

3. Do you feel your ministry team has achieved a good balance between the work that is accomplished and how it is accomplished? What specific evidence can you cite to support your assessment?

_____

_____

_____

_____

■ DISCUSSION MODULE 1.2
STRATEGIC VERSUS OPERATIONS PERFORMANCE

In assessing their own personal productivity and performance, managers often overlook strategic contributions—how their productivity advances the organization's overall mission. Organizations tend to stress the pursuit of personal job goals more than overall corporate goals.

This is understandable considering the difficulty of measuring how each individual contributes to the performance of the total mission. Nonetheless, ministry managers must never lose sight of the spiritual purpose of their Christian organization. Jobs have a tendency to take on a bureaucratic "life of their own" when not linked to a larger strategic plan.

Bureaucracy—the form of organization based on rigid procedures, multiple levels of authority, and commitment to the status quo—inevitably results when people lose sight of overall strategy and focus narrowly on their own job descriptions. More than any other type of organization, Christian ministries must stress job mission and vision.

People throughout the ministry must understand how their individual work advances the cause. The more they identify with what the ministry is striving to accomplish, the greater their individual contributions can be. By "catching the strategic vision," ministry members will be more motivated and stronger team members.

▲ SITUATION REVIEW 1.2
OPERATIONS VERSUS STRATEGIC ORIENTATION

1. To what extent has your ministry carefully clarified and communicated its strategic mission and purpose? In what specific ways has this been done?

   _____

   _____

   _____

   _____

   _____

2. Do the people you work with seem to share a sense of vision and purpose? Do they seem to identify with the overall ministry more

than their individual roles and job descriptions?

_____

_____

_____

_____

_____

3. Would you characterize the organization of your ministry as bureaucratic? Is it cumbersome and time-consuming to get decisions
made? Are you often straitjacketed by inflexible rules and procedures? Is it difficult to bring about beneficial change?

_____

_____

_____

_____

_____

4. Do you feel your own work makes direct, significant contributions
to the vision and purpose of your ministry? How?

_____

_____

_____

_____

_____

● ACTION PLAN 1.2
DEVELOPING GREATER STRATEGIC EMPHASIS

1. Identify three steps you can take to help coworkers think strategically (identify with the ministry's overall mission) rather than in terms of operations (personal job descriptions and procedures):

   A. _____

   _____

   _____

   B. _____

   _____

   _____

   C. _____

   _____

   _____

2. Define the purpose of your ministry in fewer than fifty words:

   _____

   _____

   _____

   _____

   _____

3. List three constructive things you can do in the next six months to help make your part of the organization less bureaucratic:

   A. _____

   _____

B. _____

_____

C. _____

_____

4. List three constructive things others in your ministry can do to "bust the bureaucracy":

A. _____

_____

B. _____

_____

C. _____

_____

■ DISCUSSION MODULE 1.3
TASK VERSUS PEOPLE ORIENTATION

Managers function to achieve results working through people, so there is a *task* side and a *people* side in managing. Both are equally important, yet most managers have a difficult time keeping them balanced.

Some managers tend to focus on productivity more than relationships; others overemphasize the relational side. To be professionally effective, managers must strive to balance the two orientations by interacting with coworkers in such a way that productivity naturally results. The key is developing productivity through building relationships; the two go hand in hand.

Since people are both the end and means of Christian ministry, the ministry manager must avoid two traps: abusing people while achieving results; achieving results which do not greatly benefit people. Managers heavily overbalanced toward productivity sometimes unintentionally grind people up in their drive to meet deadlines, maintain high economic efficiency, and surpass standards. Such "slave-driving" tendencies reflect a myopic sense of ministry vision, for how can one pursue human-welfare ends while using means detrimental to people?

Managers overbalanced toward interaction and relationships are apt to fall into the trap of achieving results that have meager potential for benefiting others. So much time and energy are spent by ministry members in "fellowshipping" and "ministering" to one another that little is left over for those the team is supposed to serve!

▲ SITUATION REVIEW 1.3
ASSESSMENT OF PRODUCTIVITY OVERBALANCE

Check which of the following characterize your temperament or ministry management style:

_____ 1. I dislike disruptions when I'm working.
_____ 2. I want to have a close, friendly relationship with the people with whom I work.
_____ 3. I am usually very conscious of time while working.
_____ 4. Being part of a team effort is important to me.
_____ 5. I prefer not to be very dependent on others in my work.
_____ 6. I often go out of my way to meet new people.
_____ 7. I am most productive when working alone.
_____ 8. I have a lot of friends and close acquaintances.
_____ 9. I tend to measure success by my personal achievement.
_____ 10. I usually find working with others to be stimulating.

The more odd-numbered items you checked in the above list, the more you probably tend to be *task-driven* as a manager. The even-numbered items characterize the *relationship-oriented* manager. Knowing your tendency is half the battle in balancing it!

● ACTION PLAN 1.3
BALANCING PEOPLE AND PRODUCTIVITY

1. If Situation Review 1.3 indicated you are overbalanced toward task productivity, fill out the following action plan steps:

   A. Indicate several ways you can productively interact with co-workers more frequently throughout the work day:

   _____

   _____

   _____

   _____

   B. List possible ways you can enhance your own productivity by interacting more frequently with coworkers:

   _____

   _____

   _____

   _____

   C. List the goals of your ministry which you cannot achieve by working alone:

   _____

   _____

   _____

   _____

   _____

D. Note ways in which you can enhance the productivity of your coworkers by making a greater effort to "build yourself" into them:

_____

_____

_____

_____

_____

2. If you were overbalanced toward relationships in Situation Review 1.3, the following action plan steps should help you to correct your excesses:

A. List several ways in which you can hold yourself more accountable for productivity during the workday, especially as you work in a team setting:

_____

_____

_____

_____

_____

B. List ways in which you can hold your coworkers more accountable for overall team accomplishment:

_____

_____

_____

_____

_____

C. What work can you do while you are alone to enhance the productivity of coworkers when you do interact with them?

_____

_____

_____

_____

_____

_____

D. What can members of your work team do to enhance the team's productivity?

_____

_____

_____

_____

_____

_____

■ DISCUSSION MODULE 1.4
TIME MANAGEMENT

The manager's scarcest resource is usually not information, nor manpower, nor even money—it's time. We all have exactly the same amount of it each day, but some of us have a great deal more to show for it. The goal of managing time is not to get more of it, but rather to get more out of it.

Volumes of excellent readings about time management have appeared in recent years, offering a valuable array of time-saving techniques and tips. When boiled down, however, most of this material has a common theme: control your priorities.

We spend our time according to what is most important to us. The

key to effective time management lies with carefully defining our priorities, both professional and personal. Time management is actually
priorities management—the proverbial putting first things first.

The ministry manager's priorities should revolve around the following foundational question: Who benefits by the way you spend your
time? Time management decisions in a Christian setting must be gov-
erned by the opportunity to serve others. Time invested in ministry
activities that benefit others is time well spent.

This suggests a foundational truth about effective time management:
*Since ministry managers are service-oriented, their time actually belongs
to others.* Time must not be selfishly hoarded by the manager, but
rather generously invested in others. Spending our precious time on
others is actually a greater sacrifice than spending our money on them.

The familiar adage, you have to give up something in order to get
something, rings true for time management. One of the most common
and debilitating mistakes ministry managers make is to create more
time for serving others simply by working longer hours. They seek to
serve by adding on more and more "floors" to an already towering
"skyscraper" of daily activities.

Becoming an overcommitted "workaholic" is not the solution to the
time problem. Giving up some lower priority time-consuming activities
is the only effective solution. In short, you must give up something (of
lesser importance) to get something (of greater importance). Christians who genuinely desire to serve others will strive to be
undercommitted rather than overcommitted. They will have time on
their hands, giving them a receptiveness that invites rather than shuts
out others.

Such advice may sound like sheer madness to the busiest of managers who blame "role overload" for their habitual lack of time. Indeed,
ministry managers are often extremely busy and pressed for time. But
when this becomes a professional lifestyle, a significant reworking of
time management is warranted. The Situation Review and Action Plan
that follow should prove helpful.

▲ SITUATION REVIEW 1.4
TIME TRAPS

1. Listed below are the most common managerial time wasters. Indicate how often you find yourself falling into each time trap by
   placing one of the following numbers by each item:
   2 = Frequent time trap for me
   1 = Occasional time trap
   0 = Infrequent time trap

_____ 1. Attending meetings of marginal importance to you.

_____ 2. Dealing with unscheduled drop-in visitors who primarily want to socialize or pursue low priority matters.

_____ 3. Handling telephone interruptions dealing with routine business.

_____ 4. Performing busy work that could be readily delegated (including word processing and computer chores).

_____ 5. Mixing personal pursuits with professional duties (e.g., running personal errands while at lunch, handling family matters over the phone).

_____ 6. Handling the same paperwork (memos, reports, minutes) multiple times.

_____ 7. Fumbling around to locate misfiled documents or misplaced information.

_____ 8. Explaining routine information to coworkers personally rather than via memo or meeting.

_____ 9. Overanalyzing or overdeliberating about relatively inconsequential decisions.

_____ 10. Waiting on others (for appointments, to provide information, to complete assignments).

If your total score for all ten items exceeds 10 you probably need to make a major effort to better manage your time.

2. Assess your tendency toward overcommitment by indicating how strongly you agree with each of the following statements (2 = strongly agree; 1 = mildly agree; 0 = disagree).

_____ 1. It is not unusual for me to feel overloaded with work at various times during the week.

_____ 2. It is difficult for people to get to see me without an appointment.

_____ 3. I sometimes miss work completion deadlines because I have too much to do.

_____ 4. I don't say "no" often enough when people ask me to participate in nonessential or low priority professional activities.

_____ 5. I sometimes desire to isolate myself from others in order to completely devote myself to work.

_____ 6. I occasionally "cut corners" in the way I perform my work in order to meet deadlines and get things off my desk.

_____ 7. I am sometimes hard to get along with because of work-related stresses and strains.

If your total score for the above questions exceeds 7, you may be overcommitted and in need of a more disciplined approach to managing your professional priorities and lifestyle.

● ACTION PLAN 1.4
GETTING MORE OUT OF YOUR TIME

1. Keep a time log during a typical work week. Itemize the major and
   minor activities you engaged in daily and the approximate amount
   of time spent on each. Determine about what percentage of your
   time that week was spent on each activity category. Use the
   following generic table as a guide to developing a more tailor-made
   time utilization chart for yourself. Indicate actual percentage of
   time spent versus a desired target percentage.

Percentage of Weekly Time		Activity
Spent	Desired	
____%	____%	Working by yourself.
____%	____%	Working one-on-one with others.
____%	____%	Working with a group.
____%	____%	Low priority activities.
____%	____%	Waiting for others.
____%	____%	Meals and breaks.
____%	____%	Telephone conversations.
____%	____%	Getting ready to work (e.g., gathering information, organizing desk).
____%	____%	Nonwork-related socializing.
____%	____%	Personal pursuits (errands, hobbies).
____%	____%	Performing tasks you could delegate to others.
____%	____%	Commuting from home to your work area.
____%	____%	Planning.
____%	____%	Written communication.

2. List below the five people or groups of people ("constituents") you
   invest most of your time in. Indicate the approximate percentage
   of work time you spend with each person or group and how important each is to the goals and mission of your ministry (A = very
   important; B = somewhat important; C = low in importance).

Percentage of Time Spent	Importance to Ministry	Person or Group
____	____	1.
____	____	2.
____	____	3.

		4.
		5.

Are you satisfied with the relationship between the two columns (most time spent with most important ministry constituents)? What actions can you take to achieve a better match between importance of constituents and time invested in them?

_____

_____

_____

_____

_____

■ DISCUSSION MODULE 1.5
STRESS AND BURNOUT

Stress is the price managers pay for working too hard, too long, or under too much pressure. It is inevitable that ministry managers will occasionally succumb to stress. But when that stress is prolonged and integrated into the manager's lifestyle, burnout results. Its consequences are chronic fatigue, psychosomatic disorders, and the straining of relationships.

Excess is the root of most job-related stress. Excessive work, worry, dependency, or expectations can equal stress. While work, achievement, and excellence are all worthy pursuits, when carried too far they become traps for the unwary ministry manager. Herein lies the insidious trap of stress. It results from too much of a good thing—too much work, interaction, and self-sacrifice. Managing excess is the key to managing stress.

Why do so many ministry managers overdo things and bring unnecessary stress upon themselves? Two root causes are common, and both are preventable. Many times stress is simply the by-product of poor work habits: trying to do two things at the same time (conversing on the phone while working at the computer keyboard); doing tomorrow's work today; eating on the run, and so forth.

Another core cause of stress is psychological in nature. Far too many managers, particularly those in serving professions, subconsciously define their self-worth in terms of job accomplishments. The harder they work, the more they validate their own self-worth. Unfortunately, such a spiritually myopic perspective naturally generates a "success-through-excess" syndrome. The workaholic lifestyle that results becomes extremely addictive, and stress is the inevitable hangover.

The following Situation Review can help the ministry manager gauge the presence of stress and isolate its causes.

▲ SITUATION REVIEW 1.5
STRESS ALERT

Respond to each of the following questions with a 2 for "strongly agree," a 1 for "mildly agree," and a 0 for "disagree."

_____ 1. I gain immense satisfaction from work.
_____ 2. I spend little time with escapist hobbies.
_____ 3. When working on a project, I generally strive for close-to-perfection results rather than "good enough" results.
_____ 4. My job is often very fragmented—lots of "starts and stops," interruptions, and unexpected turns.
_____ 5. I stay busy, even rushed, much of the time at work.
_____ 6. I have to depend on others to quite an extent in order to achieve job goals.
_____ 7. I have a fairly strong dislike of conflict and disagreement.
_____ 8. I often find it draining to work with others rather than by myself.
_____ 9. My need for professional security and certainty is fairly high.
_____ 10. I often take my job home with me and dwell on my work when away from the workplace.

If your total score for the above questions is much over 10, your ministry work environment probably has a high potential for stress. The following Action Plan will likely come in handy.

● ACTION PLAN 1.5
STRESS-COPING STRATEGY

1. Identify three to five "busywork" (low priority) activities you could readily remove from your weekly work routine (via delegation, better organization, or lowering of self-imposed productivity expectations), thereby making your job a bit less hectic:

A. _____

B. _____

C. _____

D. _____

E. _____

2. Identify two or three simple ways to relax that could help you relieve tension during busy work days. Consider such practices as taking short walks, varying your lunch routine, and mini-Bible devotionals at your desk.

A. _____

B. _____

C. _____

3. In what areas of your ministry work do you feel most dependent on others (and thus most vulnerable):

A. _____

B. _____

C. _____

4. What actions can you take to increase the amount of trust and team spirit you share with those you most depend upon in day-to-day situations?

_____

_____

_____

_____

_____

_____

5. In what ways can you define success more by the accomplishments of your team rather than by your own personal achievements?

_____

_____

_____

_____

_____

_____

6. Over a week's time, make note of when you feel most under stress and strive to identify what factors seem to cause these feelings. Are they tied to the type of work you do? Are they related to the way you do your work? Do the people you work with cause these feelings? Is the way people work with you a source of discomfort?

_____

_____

_____

_____

_____

_____

7. List the factors you would most like to change about the way you do your work or about how your organization operates.

_____

_____

_____

_____

_____

_____

8. What can you do to better adjust to your job situation in the absence of the ideal changes expressed in your preceding answer?

_____

_____

_____

_____

_____

_____

RESOURCES ON PERSONAL ORGANIZATION AND PRODUCTIVITY

Dayton, Edward R. *Tools for Time Management.* Grand Rapids: Zondervan Publishing House, 1974.

Douglas, Stephen; Cook, Bruce; and Hendricks, Howard. *The Ministry of Management.* Arrowhead Springs, San Bernardino, Calif.: Here's Life Publishers, 1981.

Ecker, Richard E. *The Stress Myth.* Downers Grove, Ill.: InterVarsity Press, 1985.

Engstrom, Ted W., and Dayton, Edward R. *The Christian Leaders 60-Second Management Guide.* Waco, Texas: Word, Inc., 1984.

McDonough, Reginald M. *Leading Your Church In Long Range Planning.* Nashville: Convention Press, 1975.

Morgan, John S., and Philip, J.R. *You Can't Manage Alone.* Grand Rapids: Zondervan Publishing House, 1985.

Perry, Lloyd. *Getting The Church On Target*. Chicago: Moody Press, 1977.

Porter, Mark. *The Time Of Your Life*. Wheaton, Ill.: Victor Books, 1983.

Rush, Myron. *Management: A Biblical Approach*. Wheaton, Ill.: Victor Books, 1978.

Szarejko, Francis. *How To Manage Yourself And Others*. Plainfield, N.J.: Logos International, 1979.

White, Robert N. *Managing Today's Church*. Valley Forge, Pa.: Judson Press, 1981.

Williams, George M. *Improving Parish Management*. Mystic, Conn.: Twenty-Third Publications, 1983.

MEDITATIONS FOR GOAL-SETTING

As in water face reflects face, so the heart of man reflects man (Proverbs 27:19).

Ask, and it shall be given to you; seek and you shall find; knock, and it shall be opened to you. For every one who asks receives, and he who seeks finds, and to him who knocks it shall be opened (Matthew 7:7-8).

Then He said to His disciples, "The harvest is plentiful, but the workers are few" (Matthew 9:37).

Do not merely look out for your own personal interests, but also for the interests of others (Philippians 2:4).

But speaking the truth in love, we are to grow up in all aspects into Him, who is the head, even Christ, from whom the whole body, being fitted and held together by that which every joint supplies, according to the proper working of each individual part, causes the growth of the body for the building up of itself in love (Ephesians 4:15-16).

Chapter 2

Resources for Goal-Setting

■ DISCUSSION MODULE 2.1
MAKING GOALS WORK FOR YOU

Some people dread goal-setting because goals make them feel conspicuous. ("Everyone will know what I'm supposed to be doing and whether or not I succeed in doing it!") Others have a negative reaction to goal-setting because of past experiences with an insensitive boss who autocratically imposed goals on them or used goals as a whip to drive performance. Still others sneer at goals because they have seen their organization set goals every year and then quickly forget about them.

The challenge of goal-setting is not merely to formulate goals; it is to make goals, and the whole goal-setting process, work for the organization and its members. Goals should be "friendly."

When managed effectively, goal-setting can be a strong motivating force within the Christian organization. This is because goals give people a sense of united purpose, channeling their energy in productive directions. Goals serve as performance standards, providing ministry team members with a rudder to guide daily job activities. Goals also let people know which ends and means will be endorsed and sanctioned by the organization.

In the absence of strategic goals, ministries must pay the price of slackened motivation, wasted energy, and inferior productivity. To say the least, goals are one of the most important items in any manager's tool kit.

▲ SITUATION REVIEW 2.1
GOALS: FRIEND OR FOE?

Have each member of your ministry team, including yourself, respond to the following statements. Where they strongly agree with the statement, they should put down a 2; mildly agree = 1; disagree = 0.

_____ 1. Goals make me uncomfortable because they put me under unwelcome pressure to perform.

_____ 2. I am well aware of the overall goals of my ministry.

_____ 3. I am well aware of the goals for my specific job within the ministry.

_____ 4. My job goals provide me with a great deal of direction for my daily work. They keep me on track.

_____ 5. My supervisor seems to be more concerned with goal-setting than with goal achievement.

_____ 6. I am held accountable for achieving my goals.

_____ 7. I feel my job activities are strongly endorsed and supported by my organization.

_____ 8. Goals help me be more productive.

Each team member should total the score for statements 2–4 and 6–8, which represent effective management practices. Then total the score for statements 1 and 5, which are ineffective management practices. Take the difference between the two totals. For team members scoring under 6 or 7, it would probably be worthwhile to discuss the benefits of being more goal-directed. Action Plan 2.1 will help in this effort.

● ACTION PLAN 2.1
PUTTING GOALS TO WORK

1. Have members of your ministry team list individually what they feel are the three most important goals of the ministry. List your own view of the three most important goals in the space that follows:

A.

B.

C.

2. Gather together the goal lists from your ministry team and answer the following questions:

A. To what extent do team members seem to agree on the goals of the overall ministry?

_____

_____

_____

_____

_____

B. How much do the other goal statements agree with your own list?

_____

_____

_____

_____

_____

C. What can you and ministry members do to bring about greater
    goal consensus?

_____

_____

_____

_____

_____

3. Have team members list goals for their own individual jobs. List
    your own job-specific goals in the following space:

_____

_____

_____

_____

_____

4. To what extent do you feel the job-related goals of individual team
    members support and promote overall ministry goals? In what
    ways could the two sets of goals be better integrated?

_____

_____

_____

_____

■ DISCUSSION MODULE 2.2
OPERATIONAL GOALS

Intentions are not goals. Many ministry managers confuse having a
sense of purpose for goal-setting. Merely wanting something to be

accomplished will not bring it about. An operational goal is a specific course of action that results in a measurable outcome. A goal is not operational unless it clearly specifies both ends and means.

Well-formulated ministry goals energize team members for action by giving them an exciting destination to travel toward and a road map to follow. Operational goals point where the ministry is heading and tell us when we have arrived at the final destination. Such goals show us how to start, how to measure progress, and when we have succeeded.

"Operationalizing" goals is a five-step process:
1. Describing what the end state will look like and who will benefit when it is reached.
2. Defining major completion steps that will culminate in goal attainment.
3. Setting completion deadlines for each step.
4. Selling team members on both the ends and means of the goal.
5. Implementing the goal in a proactive manner.

The following Situation Review and Action Plan amplify on these five steps.

▲ SITUATION REVIEW 2.2
ASSESSING GOALS

1. In the space below state the major goals of your ministry:

_____

_____

_____

_____

_____

_____

_____

_____

2. Review each major ministry goal using the following questions:
Ministry goal:

A. Take some time to reflect on how this particular goal was set. To what extent does it reflect the result of authentic team consensus?

_____

_____

_____

_____

B. Why is this goal necessary? Does it concern a genuine need of the ministry or only a "want"?

_____

_____

_____

_____

_____

C. What will happen if this goal is not achieved?

_____

_____

_____

_____

D. Is there any evidence that people in your ministry are excited and enthusiastic about this goal?

_____

_____

_____

_____

_____

_____

● ACTION PLAN 2.2
SETTING OPERATIONAL GOALS

Review each of the ministry goals you listed in number 1 of Situation
Review 2.2 using the questions below.
Ministry goal:

1. How will your ministry team know when you have successfully
achieved this goal?

_____

_____

_____

_____

_____

_____

2. Who will benefit when this goal is achieved? How will they benefit?

_____

_____

_____

_____

_____

_____

3. What major subgoals must be reached before the final goal can be attained?

_____

_____

_____

_____

_____

4. When must each subgoal be achieved to keep the project on target toward completion?

_____

_____

_____

_____

_____

5. What hurdles and "brushfires" might you encounter in implementing this goal?

_____

_____

_____

_____

_____

6. What actions can you take beforehand to prevent or minimize anticipated obstacles?

_____

_____

_____

_____

_____

7. How can team members encourage and support one another while the goal is being implemented?

_____

_____

_____

_____

_____

■ DISCUSSION MODULE 2.3
MANAGEMENT BY OBJECTIVES

"Management by objectives" (MBO) is a familiar concept to most managers, even if they've never used it. MBO is a formal, written process designed to involve subordinates in goal-setting and hold them accountable for their performance. A number of books and articles, including some from a Christian perspective, explain the process.

Ministry managers would be wise to use MBO with discretion however, since it is easily abused. This stems from MBO's fundamental emphasis on performance. Under a typical MBO system, people are valued more for what they do than for who they are. Obviously, professional performance is vitally important to all organizations, but should it be the driving force of Christian ministries?

Christians are called to value people _for who they are_ (spiritually), not merely _for what they produce_ (economically). This is not always easy to do in our materialistic Western culture, yet it is essential that managers view team members as more than mere factors of production.

Situation Review 2.3 and Action Plan 2.3 present the concept of "management by mission" (MBM) as an alternative to management by objectives. MBM focuses on the unique niches occupied by members of the ministry team. People are valued because of their special place in the ministry "family," not merely because they achieve goals and meet deadlines. Belonging is emphasized along with producing, although producing is a natural byproduct of belonging.

▲ SITUATION REVIEW 2.3
ROLE ASSESSMENT

Have each member of your ministry team respond to the following questions, and then discuss the responses as a group.

1. To what extent does your ministry team have a sense of "family"?

_____

_____

_____

_____

_____

2. Do you feel you occupy a unique niche on your ministry team? If so, what is your niche?

_____

_____

_____

_____

_____

3. What unique roles do other team members fill?

_____

_____

_____

_____

_____

4. In what respects are you valued by your team?

_____

_____

_____

_____

5. How would members of your team probably respond if your own personal productivity were to decline significantly? How would it affect their work habits?

_____

_____

_____

_____

● **ACTION PLAN 2.3**
MANAGEMENT BY MISSION

Team members should respond to the following statements individually and then meet one-on-one with the ministry manager to develop personalized ministry goals.

1. Ideally I would like to have the following role or niche on my ministry team:

_____

_____

_____

_____

_____

2. These are the primary contributions I can make to my ministry team:

_____

_____

_____

_____

_____

3. These are the areas where I most need support and assistance from the other members of my ministry team:

_____

_____

_____

_____

_____

4. Here are ways we could better work together as a team:

_____

_____

_____

_____

_____

5. I could increase my contributions to the team if the following
things occurred:

_____

_____

_____

_____

_____

_____

6. I want to improve my personal performance in the following measurable ways:

_____

_____

_____

_____

_____

_____

7. I feel the ministry would benefit if the following changes were
made by others:

_____

_____

_____

_____

_____

RESOURCES FOR GOAL-SETTING

Allison, Joseph D. *Setting Goals That Count.* Grand Rapids: Zondervan Publishing House, 1977.

Cook, William H. *Success, Motivation, And The Scriptures.* Nashville: Broadman Press, 1974.

Getz, Gene A. *Sharpening The Focus Of The Church.* Wheaton, Ill.: Victor Books, 1984.

Howard, J. Grant. *Balancing Life's Demands: A New Perspective On Priorities.* Portland: Multnomah Press, 1983.

Johnston, Jon. *Christian Excellence—Alternative to Success.* Grand Rapids: Baker Book House, 1985.

Knudsen, Raymond B. *New Models For Church Administration.* Chicago: Follett Press, 1979.

Morgan, John S., and Philip, J.R. *You Can't Manage Alone.* Grand Rapids: Zondervan Publishing House, 1985.

Perry, Lloyd. *Getting The Church On Target.* Chicago: Moody Press, 1977.

Tidwell, Charles A. *Church Administration—Effective Leadership For Ministry.* Nashville: Broadman Press, 1985.

MEDITATIONS FOR PLANNING AND CONTROLLING

The way of a fool is right in his own eyes, but a wise man is he who listens to counsel (Proverbs 12:15).

Without consultation, plans are frustrated, but with many counselors they succeed (Proverbs 15:22).

Commit your works to the Lord, and your plans will be established (Proverbs 16:3).

Like a city that is broken into and without walls is a man who has no control over his spirit (Proverbs 25:28).

Therefore every one who hears these words of Mine, and acts upon them, may be compared to a wise man, who built his house upon the rock. And the rain descended, and the floods came, and the winds blew, and burst against that house; and yet it did not fall, for it had been founded upon the rock. And everyone who hears these words of Mine, and does not act upon them, will be like a foolish man, who built his house upon the sand. And the rain descended, and the floods came, and the winds blew, and burst against that house, and it fell, and great was its fall (Matthew 7:24-27).

Chapter 3

Resources for Planning and Control

■ DISCUSSION MODULE 3.1
PLANNING IN PERSPECTIVE

Planning is the process of turning vision into reality—of making things happen the way you and your ministry team desire. Planning is very much a partnership between you and God in which supernatural power can be channeled through the human efforts of a committed ministry team.

It is for this reason that planning is both proactive (making things happen) and reactive (waiting for them to happen). The key challenge in planning is to maintain the right balance between acting and reacting—between human effort and divine intervention.

Planning should concentrate more on ministry effectiveness (doing the right things) than efficiency (doing things in the "right" way). This means the planning process begins by focusing on the ministry's basic mission (ultimate purpose), which is the very foundation of effectiveness. From here, planning must encompass the other broad components of effectiveness: *goals* (specific outcomes to be attained by the ministry); *strategy* (the broad "game plan" for achieving those goals); and *tactics* (successful implementation of the game plan). Action Plan 3.1 provides you with a planning framework for all three effectiveness levels.

The process of planning is actually more important than the specific plans themselves. In the final analysis, planning is valuable because it facilitates ministry communication, vision-sharing, and team member interaction. It is these interpersonal processes that actually fuel ministry progress and effectiveness. Planning is the catalyst for team accomplishment.

▲ SITUATION REVIEW 3.1
HOW SOLID IS YOUR PLANNING FOUNDATION?

1. How often do you get together as team members to pray for the needs of the ministry?

_____

_____

2. At a typical planning session with your team, what percentage of the time do you discuss the purpose and mission of your ministry rather than implementation activities?

_____

_____

_____

3. To what extent does planning in your ministry serve as a catalyst for teamwork? Do you see it helping people to smoothly work together? How do your planning efforts sometimes unintentionally constrain and hinder the team by limiting people's enthusiasm and creativity?

_____

_____

_____

_____

4. Do you feel your ministry team usually achieves a satisfactory balance between proactive planning and reactive planning? How do the other members of your ministry team feel about this?

_____

_____

_____

_____

_____

5. Do members of your ministry team regularly spend time planning how they can work together more productively?

_____

_____

_____

● ACTION PLAN 3.1
FOUNDATION WORK

1. Develop three goals for forming a more solid partnership with God in planning for your ministry and ministry team:

Goal 1: _____
Goal 2: _____
Goal 3: _____

2. List several actions you can take at your next team meeting to better focus members on the ministry's mission and goals (and to avoid getting completely caught up in implementation details):

_____

_____

_____

_____

_____

3. List several things your team will try to make happen in the next year:

_____

_____

_____

_____

_____

4. In what ways will waiting help you achieve the proactive planning goals listed in number 3? Discuss how your team can "wait for success" as well as "make success."

_____

_____

_____

_____

_____

■ **DISCUSSION MODULE 3.2**
ORGANIC PLANNING

Planning is never a finished process. It has no clearcut beginning or end. Rather, planning continuously evolves and unfolds, shaped by events both inside and outside the ministry. One writer has compared planning to a butterfly in flight: seemingly erratic yet moving inexorably toward a destination.

This organic planning process of starts and stops and roundabout progress requires great patience and discernment. Progress rarely comes as fast as the team wants or exactly in the way envisioned. Unanticipated mid-course corrections are inevitable, and team members won't always feel in complete control.

Experienced managers, knowing they are not masters of their destinies, learn to cope with the proactive/reactive nature of organic planning by cultivating team flexibility and openness to change. Rather than naively assuming that ministry planning can somehow be mastered and controlled, effective managers instead concentrate on the process of planning: keeping in close touch with ministry members and activities, communicating the vision, and building cooperative relationships on the team.

A recent bestseller on managing likens planning to the delicate process of steering a sailboat by rudder—the wind and sea can never be mastered but their powerful energy can be productively harnessed. Neither can ministry teams master the many forces that influence planning, but they can learn to harness these forces in reaching goals.

▲ SITUATION REVIEW 3.2
ASSESSING PLANNING FLEXIBILITY

1. Is your ministry team patient in its planning? Cite specific recent examples of such patience:

_____

_____

_____

_____

_____

2. Give examples of planning flexibility in your ministry—of your capacity to adjust, adapt, re-evaluate, and change.

_____

_____

_____

_____

_____

3. In what ways has your team been inflexible and slow to change?

_____

_____

_____

_____

_____

4. Is your team failing to harness its potential because of shortcomings in relationships among team members? How is this occurring?

_____

_____

_____

_____

_____

● ACTION PLAN 3.2
PLANNING CALISTHENICS

1. List three goals your ministry is currently planning for. For each goal, discuss how your team can display planning patience (how you can wait for things to happen in addition to making them happen):

Goal 1:

Patience: _____

_____

Goal 2:

Patience: _____

_____

_____

Goal 3:

Patience: _____

_____

_____

2. In light of the three ministry goals listed above, discuss how your team's planning flexibility can be enhanced through the following means:

A. Anticipating implementation problems before they occur:

_____

_____

_____

_____

B. Focusing on how others outside the ministry will benefit from your team's pursuit of goals:

_____

_____

_____

_____

C. Emphasizing effectiveness (mission consciousness) over efficiency (ease of implementation):

_____

_____

_____

_____

3. Are there ways in which relationships between two or more members of the team can be strengthened, better coordinated, or more creatively managed?

_____

_____

_____

_____

_____

4. Set three goals for enhancing planning flexibility through strengthening how team members interact with one another:

Goal 1:

Goal 2:

Goal 3:

■ DISCUSSION MODULE 3.3
TWO-WAY PLANNING

Who should be a part of the planning process? A simple rule of thumb applies: those directly affected by ministry plans should be involved in the planning. Many managers see planning in a more limited way, preferring to involve as few people as possible to expedite time efficiency and minimize conflict. The resulting "top down" planning approach does proceed efficiently, but rarely effectively. Over time, the myopic top-down planner will sadly discover that lack of team participation inevitably leads to lack of commitment.

Top-down, or unilateral, planning places too much emphasis on developing plans and not enough on implementing them. Yet planning success rests more with how plans are implemented than with how they are conceived. Plans "hatched" in isolation stand little chance of being enthusiastically and thoughtfully implemented.

Bilateral (or two-way) planning, involving continuous dialogue between ministry leaders and team members, is much more likely to succeed because it nurtures a fertile planning climate: listening, learning, compromising, clarifying, encouraging, and challenging. When team members work together in formulating plans, they will also work together in implementing them. Both the "content" and process dimensions of planning can thus be satisfied.

Just as there are different roles on the ministry team, there are different roles for team members to play in the planning process. Certain members will be information providers, others will be information processors, still others will share and disseminate information. Some will provide technical expertise in planning, others will use interpersonal and persuasive skills, while others will "troubleshoot" implementation activities.

Ministry leaders should do everything possible to make team members feel uniquely useful in planning for ministry success. In this way, they will feel they "own" the ministry plan and are personally accountable for its success.

▲ SITUATION REVIEW 3.3
UNILATERAL OR BILATERAL?

Have the members of your ministry team state how much they agree with each of the following statements, where 2 = strongly agree; 1 = agree; 0 = disagree.

_____ 1. Each member of my ministry team has ample opportunity to be involved in planning.

_____ 2. Our leader sometimes exerts too much influence on ministry planning.

_____ 3. My own contributions to the ministry's plans are valuable and worthwhile.

_____ 4. Team members don't participate enough in ministry planning.

_____ 5. Team members sensitively listen to one another in our planning efforts.

_____ 6. Ministry activities are not always well thought through; we sometimes go off "half-cocked."

_____ 7. Ministry planning efforts are generally very challenging and help the team overcome the status quo.

_____ 8. Ministry planning efforts often leave me discouraged and frustrated.

_____ 9. Each member of the ministry team has a distinctive, unique role to play in the planning process.

_____ 10. When we plan, we tend to focus more on implementation than on mission and goals.

Score each team member's inventory by deriving a total for the even-numbered items (poor planning practices) and a separate total for the odd-numbered (beneficial planning practices). Subtract the two totals to get the final score. Scores in the 5-or-under range indicate lack of bilateral planning. The team leader would be well-advised to address the matter at a team meeting. Action Plan 3.3 can be beneficial.

● ACTION PLAN 3.3
MAXIMIZING TEAM PLANNING

The team leader should respond to the following questions as a guide to stimulating better two-way planning:

1. Which team members tend to remain quiet at ministry planning sessions?

_____

_____

_____

2. What will you do at the next team meeting to encourage those listed in step 1 to participate more?

_____

_____

_____

_____

3. What can you do to slow down future team meetings and so create an atmosphere of more opportunity for discussion and participation?

_____

_____

_____

_____

4. List several ways in which team members have recently benefited you and enhanced ministry effectiveness:

_____

_____

_____

_____

_____

5. How can you make it easier for team members to benefit you and the ministry?

_____

_____

_____

_____

_____

■ DISCUSSION MODULE 3.4
DEVELOPING A FERTILE PLANNING CLIMATE

Since planning invariably introduces change into the ministry (new directions and goals, revised work procedures, different performance standards, new precedents), a working climate conducive to change is essential. The more team members are concerned with ministry effectiveness (mission, goals, strategy), the more they will perceive change as an opportunity for promoting ministry success.

People concerned primarily with ministry efficiency (procedures, rules, budgets) are often change resistant, creating a less fertile climate for planning. Efficiency-oriented people are apt to accommodate the status quo in planning, creating a difficult climate for achievement. Action Plan 3.4 provides specific action guidelines for emphasizing planning effectiveness.

▲ SITUATION REVIEW 3.4
PLANNING FERTILITY

At a meeting, have members reach a consensus on which of the following characterize your ministry's planning environment. Place a check by each item that characterizes the ministry's planning approach.

——— 1. Openness to change and willingness to break with tradition.
——— 2. Mutual encouragement.
——— 3. Learning from one another.
——— 4. Constructive disagreement or criticism.
——— 5. Open-minded listening.
——— 6. Objective analysis free of emotional bias.
——— 7. Challenging one another toward heightened performance.
——— 8. Willingness to engage in beneficial compromise.
——— 9. Willingness to forgive mistakes and bear patiently with one
          another.
——— 10. Expressed mutual appreciation and positive reinforcement.
——— 11. Perceiving change as a positive opportunity.
——— 12. Cooperative spirit while implementing planning changes.

● ACTION PLAN 3.4
IMPROVING THE PLANNING ENVIRONMENT

1. Have team members discuss, as constructively as possible, why
certain items in Situation Review 3.4 were not checked. Summa-
rize their perspective in the following space:

_____

_____

_____

_____

_____

2. How would ministry performance be enhanced if the team could
improve on the unchecked items in Situation Review 3.4?

_____

_____

_____

_____

_____

3. As a team, re-evaluate each characteristic of your planning environment in light of its importance to ministry success. Rank each of the twelve items from most important to your ministry (ranked one) to least important (ranked twelve). Place rankings in the space beside each item.

Rank   Planning Environment Characteristic

_____   1. Openness to change and willingness to break with tradition.
_____   2. Mutual encouragement.
_____   3. Learning from one another.
_____   4. Constructive disagreement or criticism.
_____   5. Open-minded listening.
_____   6. Objective analysis free of emotional bias.
_____   7. Challenging one another toward heightened performance.
_____   8. Willingness to engage in beneficial compromise.
_____   9. Willingness to forgive mistakes and bear patiently with one another.
_____   10. Expressed mutual appreciation and positive reinforcement.
_____   11. Perceiving change as a positive opportunity.
_____   12. Cooperative spirit while implementing planning changes.

■ DISCUSSION MODULE 3.5
BRUSHFIRE MANAGEMENT

Many managers stay so busy "putting out brushfires" (resolving unexpected problems) that they can find little time for planning. Ironically, brushfire management is caused by this very lack of planning! In the absence of planning, managers frequently end up as victims of circumstances and control is largely lost.

Preventive maintenance is the key to avoiding brushfires. Most managerial problems can be prevented, or largely neutralized, with planning. On a formal basis, preventive maintenance takes the form of well-thought-out policies, procedures, rules and other "standing plans" which managers use for daily direction. These formal plans help insure that team members all play by the same rules, thereby reducing opportunity for administrative confusion, miscommunication, and sloppy coordination.

On a more informal (spontaneous behavior) basis, preventive maintenance is bolstered by interpersonal rapport between team members. People who communicate with one another, appreciate one another, and understand one another can work together smoothly as a team.

They experience fewer of the disruptive interpersonal problems and tensions that fuel most brushfires. The following Situation Review and Action Plan will help the ministry manager prevent brushfires through rapport-building (an issue that is further discussed in a subsequent chapter).

▲ SITUATION REVIEW 3.5
BRUSHFIRE POTENTIAL

1. Indicate how frequently you and your team members encounter the following problems in your ministry (2 = frequently; 1 = occasionally; 0 = rarely).

_____ 1. Uncoordinated follow-through ("the right hand doesn't know what the left hand is doing").

_____ 2. Decisions made in a "vacuum" (some team members are informed of important decisions, while others remain in the dark).

_____ 3. Team meetings deal primarily with the status quo and seldom inquire about possible future events.

_____ 4. Team members are confused or poorly informed about "standard operating procedures" and don't know how to take action.

_____ 5. Team members interact frequently with one another while performing their work.

_____ 6. Team members are kept well informed about one another's job pursuits and activities.

_____ 7. Members of different teams in the organization regularly interact and "cross-pollinate."

_____ 8. Team members put the goals of their particular ministry ahead of the goals of the overall organization.

Add up your responses to statements 5–7 (factors that prevent brushfires) and subtract the total for statements 1–4 and 8 (factors that fuel brushfires). If the final score is above 5, the potential for brushfires developing in your ministry may be high. A team meeting to discuss options for preventive maintenance would probably be very worthwhile.

● ACTION PLAN 3.5
MANAGING BRUSHFIRES

As a team discuss how your ministry could take advantage of the following opportunities for improved communication and rapport:

1. Keeping team members and the overall organization better informed of team activities and pursuits:

_____

_____

_____

_____

_____

2. Reaching important decisions in less of a vacuum, with greater team member participation:

_____

_____

_____

_____

3. Increasing your team contingency planning ("what-if" plans that will automatically go into effect in the event of unexpected future events):

_____

_____

_____

_____

4. Increasing "cross-pollination" with other ministries in the organization:

_____

_____

_____

_____

_____

5. Helping team members better appreciate one another's work problems and accomplishments:

_____

_____

_____

_____

_____

6. Reducing the lack of communication about operating procedures, policies, and methodology in the ministry:

_____

_____

_____

_____

_____

■ DISCUSSION MODULE 3.6
CONTROLLING MINISTRY MANAGEMENT

Control is the most overlooked, least appreciated phase of management, yet it serves as the steering wheel of the organization. Control provides follow-up to insure that plans are more than good intentions. Not only does control facilitate plan accomplishment, it generates momentum to lift ministries out of the status quo. Lack of follow-through has side-tracked far more ministries than faulty planning.

Follow through is a process of checking performance, comparing against expectations, and correcting off-target results. Planning is the basis for all three of these. Goals formulated in the planning process become the target of control; ministry effectiveness measures provide control expectations; the bilateral planning process facilitates performance evaluation. Situation Review 3.6 and Action Plan 3.6 develop a practical framework for checking, comparing, and correcting ministry performance.

The ideal of bureaucratic managers is to create an organization that runs itself. A technique known as "management by exception" (MBE) is advocated by control-oriented managers who feel managers should actively involve themselves in an operation only when something is wrong (off target). When things are going according to plan, the MBE manager is advised to put it on "automatic pilot" and let subordinates run the show.

Management by exception does enable managers to save time, but this relates more to ministry efficiency than effectiveness. Managers who isolate themselves from team activities until something is amiss risk dampening team morale by accentuating the negative and ignoring the positive. Who wants to be perceived by subordinates as a "cloud" continually "raining on someone's parade"? Teams are built more by positive reinforcement and active interaction than by negative reinforcement and isolation!

▲ SITUATION REVIEW 3.6
MINISTRY CONTROL AUDIT

1. Check which of the following formal control techniques are used in your ministry:
_____ 1. Written budget.
_____ 2. Annual financial auditing.
_____ 3. Progress reports.
_____ 4. Cost/benefit analysis of new projects and programs (comparing anticipated costs with estimated benefits).
_____ 5. Zero-base budgeting (rejustifying budgets at the beginning of each fiscal year rather than automatically maintaining or increasing last year's budget).
_____ 6. Completion deadlines.
_____ 7. Written standards of acceptable performance or quality.
_____ 8. Job descriptions.
_____ 9. Written operating procedures.
_____ 10. Quality circles (regular team meetings to assess performance progress and troubleshoot problems).

_____ 11. Periodic financial and budget status reports.

_____ 12. "Sunset" provision (annual or biannual review of all programs to consider their ongoing feasibility).

2. Have members of the ministry team state how much they agree with the following statements (2 = strongly agree; 1 = agree; 0 = disagree).

_____ 1. I hear more from my team leader when I do something wrong than when I do something right.

_____ 2. The purpose of most of our team meetings is to discuss mistakes we've made and how to improve our performance.

_____ 3. My team leader spends a great deal of time troubleshooting ministry problems.

_____ 4. While working, I do not interact very often with my team leader.

_____ 5. I work pretty much on my own unless I run into a problem.

If many team members score higher than 4 or 5 on the statements (which are ineffective control practices) in part 2., the team leader may well be relying on management by exception. A team meeting to discuss work expectations would probably be beneficial.

● ACTION PLAN 3.6
PLANNING FOR CONTROL

1. Could your ministry be making profitable use of some of the control techniques not checked in Part 1 of Situation Review 3.6? Have your team decide which additional techniques would be most useful to the ministry.

_____

_____

_____

_____

_____

2. For each of the programs in your ministry, answer the following questions:

Program:

A. What is the major goal of this program? _____

_____

_____

_____

_____

_____

B. How will you begin to measure your progress toward attaining
   this goal?

_____

_____

_____

_____

_____

C. What is the deadline for attaining the goal? _____

_____

D. Break the goal down into subgoals and set an approximate
   completion deadline for each:

_____

_____

_____

_____

_____

E. What are the primary costs (financial and nonfinancial) of this program?

_____

_____

_____

_____

_____

F. What are the program's potential benefits to your ministry at the present?

_____

_____

_____

_____

_____

G. Based on your perception of the program's costs and benefits, how high a priority should this program receive in your ministry?

_____

_____

H. Based on the program's priority in the overall ministry, how much resource support (budget, staffing, time allocation) should it receive?

_____

_____

_____

■ DISCUSSION MODULE 3.7
HOW CONTROL GETS OUT OF CONTROL

Over-control is a common organizational disease, characterized by excessive rules, procedures, committees, and routine paperwork—in short, "paralysis by analysis." Bureaucracy results: an inflexible, hard-to-change form of organization wedded to the status quo. In bureaucracies, means (such as standard operating procedures and job descriptions) become an end in themselves, causing many team members to lose sight of their mission. Instead of striving to achieve goals, bureaucratic employees tend to focus on enforcing rules, processing paperwork, and maintaining precedent.

Control gets out of hand when team members are rewarded primarily for achieving short-run performance quotas (e.g., hours worked, meetings attended, budgets cut), rather than for progress made towards the long-term ministry mission (e.g., creative breakthroughs, team members trained and developed). Controls must serve people, not vice versa!

▲ SITUATION REVIEW 3.7
RED TAPE AUDIT

Have team members state how much they agree (2 = strongly agree; 1 = agree; 0 = disagree) with the following statements:

_____ 1. We have too many meetings around here.
_____ 2. I get frustrated by all the paperwork that goes with my job.
_____ 3. Change is very hard to bring about in this ministry.
_____ 4. There is too much low-priority, routine work in my job.
_____ 5. We have to do everything "by the book" in this organization.
_____ 6. Too many of the people I work with have an "8:00 to 5:00" mentality—put in your hours and go home.
_____ 7. Tradition and precedent ("we've always done it that way") are very important in this ministry.
_____ 8. "That can't be done," and "That will never work," are heard a lot around here.

● ACTION PLAN 3.7
BUREAUCRACY BUSTERS

Go over the statements in Situation Review 3.7 with your team. Where most of the team strongly agrees (2) or agrees (1) with a statement, answer the following questions:
Statement number _____:

1. Why do you feel this way? Is your agreement with the statement based more on facts or feelings?

_____

_____

_____

_____

_____

2. What brought about this aspect of bureaucracy in the ministry?

_____

_____

_____

_____

3. What can be done immediately to make things less bureaucratic?

_____

_____

_____

_____

4. What can be done over the long-run to lessen bureaucracy in this area:

_____

_____

_____

_____

_____

5. In what strategic ways would the ministry benefit by less bureaucratic structure?

_____

_____

_____

_____

_____

RESOURCES ON
PLANNING AND CONTROL

Cook, Bruce; Douglas, Stephen; and Hendricks, Howard. *The Ministry of Management.* Arrowhead Springs, San Bernardino, Calif.: Here's Life Publishers, 1981.

Knudson, Raymond B. *New Models For Church Administration.* Chicago: Follett Press, 1979.

Lindgren, Alvin J., and Shawchuck, Norman. *Management For Your Church.* Nashville: Organization Resources Press, 1984.

McDonough, Reginald M. *Leading Your Church In Long Range Planning.* Nashville: Convention Press, 1975.

Morgan, John S., and Philip, J.R. *You Can't Manage Alone.* Grand Rapids: Zondervan Publishing House, 1985.

Powers, Bruce P. *Church Administration Handbook.* Nashville: Broadman Press, 1985.

Rush, Myron. *Management: A Biblical Approach.* Wheaton, Ill.: Victor Books, 1978.

Tidwell, Charles A. *Church Administration Effective Leadership For Ministry*. Nashville: Broadman Press, 1985.

Walrath, Douglas A. *Planning For Your Church*. Philadelphia: Westminster Press, 1984.

White, Robert N. *Managing Today's Church*. Valley Forge, Pa.: Judson Press, 1981.

Williams, George M. *Improving Parish Management*. Mystic, Conn.: Twenty-Third Publications, 1983.

MEDITATIONS FOR DECISION-MAKING AND PROBLEM-SOLVING

Trust in the LORD with all your heart, and do not lean on your own understanding. In all your ways acknowledge Him, and He will make your paths straight. Do not be wise in your own eyes. Fear the LORD and turn away from evil. It will be healing to your body, and refreshment to your bones (Proverbs 3:5-8).

For the ways of a man are before the eyes of the LORD, and He watches all his paths (Proverbs 5:21).

And do not be conformed to this world, but be transformed by the renewing of your mind, that you may prove what the will of God is, that which is good and acceptable and perfect (Romans 12:2).

So then let us pursue the things which make for peace and the building up of one another (Romans 14:19).

Are you so foolish? Having begun by the Spirit, are you now being perfected by the flesh? (Galatians 3:3)

Chapter 4

Resources for Decision-Making and Problem-Solving

■ DISCUSSION MODULE 4.1
DECISION-MAKING: WORKING SMARTER RATHER THAN HARDER

All managers have one thing in common: they must make decisions. The reality that decisions can make or break the organization presents both an awesome challenge and opportunity, because sound decision-making is definitely the foundation of ministry success.

Though decision-making issues vary across different ministries, the process of making sound decisions remains the same—a matter of working "smarter" rather than harder. Anyone can make a decision, but not necessarily one that stands the test of time. Smart decisions are characterized by five qualities:

1. Reality-orientation
2. Cost-benefit analysis
3. Timeliness
4. Facts balanced with "feels"
5. Incrementalism

Reality-orientation: Effective decision-makers stay in close touch with such ministry realities as resource constraints, morale, team members' capabilities, and learning from mistakes. They have a good sense of what is realistic and unrealistic and how members of the ministry team perceive reality. Their "sixth-sense" feel of things comes from frequent interaction with team members—from being plugged in to team activities and fluctuating workplace circumstances. "Management by walking around" is a recently coined phrase that aptly describes this in-touch reality-orientation process.

Cost-benefit analysis: Smart decision-makers not only stay in touch, they have a knack for identifying which options will be most fruitful to pursue. This requires keen insight into the probable costs and benefits of action alternatives and an ability to make intelligent trade-offs between the two. Which costs are worth incurring to derive which benefits? Cost-benefit discernment lies with consulting ministry team members, who should always be the decision-maker's closest confidants and window on reality.

Timeliness: The third quality of smart decision-making is knowing when to make the decision. Both premature and procrastinated decisions can extract a heavy toll. Wise managers realize when more information is needed to make a decision or when additional team consultation is warranted. They also know when the costs of analyzing a decision further outweigh the benefits and "paralysis by analysis" is about to set in. Timely decision-making is the product of experience and, once again, open-minded consultation with the ministry team.

Facts balanced with "feels": Decisions result from facts and "feels," but achieving the right balance is never easy. Some managers rely too much on facts ("Mr. Spocks") while others over-rely on feelings ("Captain Kirks"). Both objective analysis and intuitive feel are involved in decision-making, even though some decisions are more "head" decisions than "heart" decisions. Whatever the nature of the decision, ministry managers must strive to blend intellect and intuition to achieve decision-making balance.

Incrementalism: Effective decision-makers learn most from acting in progressive increments—step by step, phase by phase. They resist the tendency to make important future decisions until receiving feedback on the results of related past decisions. Therefore, decisions are made in an interlocking sequence. Incrementalism thus explains why on-the-job experience promotes sound decision-making. Managers learn what works in the ministry and thus make their future decisions accordingly.

The Situation Review and the Action Plan which follow integrate the five qualities of effective decisions into a framework that promotes team interaction and participation in the decision-making process.

▲ SITUATION REVIEW 4.1
ASSESSING YOUR DECISION-MAKING STYLE

1. A. Which members of your ministry team do you consult with most consistently in reaching important decisions?

_____

_____

B. Check which of the following are major reasons why you turn to the counsel of these particular team members:

_____ I'm good friends with them.

_____ We have compatible personalities.

_____ They work hard and conscientiously.

_____ They usually agree with me.

_____ They often have information I don't have.

_____ They have competencies which I lack.

_____ They are open-minded and willing to compromise.

_____ They challenge me and hold me accountable.

_____ They are unusually enthusiastic about the work of the ministry.

_____ They are very perceptive and aware.

C. Based on an examination of your profile of checked items in question 2, check which one of the following best describes how you tend to choose counselors. Try to be as honest and objective as possible.

_____ I tend to choose people who like me and are on "my side."

_____ I choose people who can help me or do something for me.

_____ I choose people who stretch me and challenge me to grow professionally.

2. Indicate how strongly you agree with each statement below (2 = strongly agree, 1 = agree, and 0 = disagree).

_____ 1. I am often impatient for ministry results and progress.

_____ 2. I tend to look for optimum solutions to problems rather than merely satisfactory ones.

_____ 3. I make up my mind easily.

_____ 4. Before I make an important decision, I like to thoroughly analyze the issues involved.

_____ 5. I stay extremely busy most of the time.

_____ 6. I dislike conflict on the ministry team and try to avoid or minimize it.

_____ 7. I am a confident decision-maker most of the time.

_____ 8. I tend to work at a relaxed pace.

Subtract your total score for the even-numbered statements (factors that promote procrastination) from your total for the odd-numbered (factors that promote premature decision-making). The more the difference exceeds 0 (on a -8 to 8 scale), the greater the likelihood you may be a premature decision-maker. A final score around or below 0 may indicate you are a procrastinator.

3. Once again, state how strongly you agree with the following statements (2 = strongly agree, 1 = agree, 0 = disagree).

_____ 1. While working with others, I am usually very aware of how they feel.

_____ 2. Lots of information helps me make decisions.

_____ 3. I am most comfortable with decisions that involve group consensus.

_____ 4. I tend to spend more time thinking about the possible results of a decision than how people will react to it.

_____ 5. I try to avoid making unpopular decisions.

_____ 6. I don't usually have enough time to do a cost-benefit analysis of decision-making alternatives.

_____ 7. My decisions are often influenced by the mood I'm in.

_____ 8. I make few spontaneous decisions.

Subtract your total score for the even-numbered statements (intellectual decision-making) from your total for the odd-numbered (emotional decision-making). The more your subtracted difference is above 0 (-8 to 8 scale), the more you probably are influenced by your feelings in making decisions. Scores around or below 0 may indicate a more intellectual/analytical orientation to decision-making.

● ACTION PLAN 4.1
EXPANDING YOUR EFFECTIVENESS AS A DECISION-MAKER

1. A. Have your closest decision-making counselors review your results for all three parts of Situation Review 4.1. To what extent do they feel that these results accurately reflect your decision-making style? Do you agree with them?

_____

_____

_____

_____

B. What would you most like to change about your decision-making style? Why?

_____

_____

_____

_____

C. Consider the sort of day-to-day decisions that you make. What can ministry team members do to help you become a more effective decision-maker?

_____

_____

_____

_____

2. Use the following questions to guide your team in cost/benefit analysis of important decisions.

Decision under consideration:

A. Why are you making this decision? _____

_____

_____

_____

_____

_____

B. How do you know this is the right time to make it?

_____

_____

_____

_____

C. What are the major alternative courses of action associated
   with this decision?

_____

_____

_____

_____

D. For each alternative, answer the following questions:
   1. What primary benefits are offered by this alternative? Con-
      sider potential benefits to ministry team members, those
      served by the ministry, and the overall organization.

_____

_____

_____

2. How well does this alternative mesh with the mission and goals of the ministry?

3. What different types of costs are associated with this particular alternative? Consider all the following types of costs: financial, time, facilities, staff stress, and other opportunities foregone.

4. How predictable and certain are the costs and benefits identified in A and C above?

_____

_____

   5. If this alternative were selected over the others, how readi-
      ly would those served by the ministry probably accept this
      decision?

_____

_____

_____

_____

_____

_____

3. The following analysis can help your team benefit from the advantages of incremental decision-making.

   Decision under consideration:

   A. What past decisions and ministry activities led your team to
      consider this decision?

_____

_____

_____

_____

_____

   B. To what extent would the momentum of on-going ministry ac-
      tivities and programs be jeopardized if your team delayed mak-
      ing this decision?

_____

_____

_____

_____

_____

C. What future decisions will probably be prompted by making this decision?

_____

_____

_____

_____

_____

D. Is this decision the logical next step of a related decision made in the past, or is it a new initiative not closely linked to the past?

_____

_____

_____

_____

_____

E. Review the available history pertaining to the decision. To what extent has this decision been prompted by ineffective or unproductive past decisions? (Are you simply trying to "paint your way out of a corner"?)

_____

_____

_____

_____

_____

F. In what ways will this decision reinforce the effectiveness and
   success of past decisions?

_____

_____

_____

_____

_____

■ DISCUSSION MODULE 4.2
PROFILE OF THE POOR DECISION-MAKER

Much can be learned about effective decision-making from observing
characteristics of the poor decision-maker. For example, managers
who work largely in isolation of the ministry team will be out of touch
with ministry realities, producing unrealistic, hard-to-implement decisions. Managers who cannot look beyond the short-run are often myopic decision-makers, bogged down by tradition and lack of creativity.

Managers who lack goal-consciousness fail at decision-making con-
sistency and follow-through. Those who have a high need to please
everyone too often compromise away decision-making success. Un-
creative managers are doomed to repeating the mistakes of past decision-makers, while politically naive ones experience seemingly endless
roadblocks in implementing decisions.

Insecure managers who vacillate and "waffle" in sticking with decisions quickly lose credibility with team members or are simply ignored. Managers who crave decision-making certainty and duck risk-
taking probably lack imagination and innovativeness.

The profile of effective decision-makers begins to emerge. They
interact frequently with the team, keep the long-run vision in sight,
and are not wedded to the status quo. They are goal-focused, aware of
political trends in the organization, and occasionally willing to be nontraditional. Good decision-makers also understand the difference between being liked and being respected.

▲ SITUATION REVIEW 4.2
GAUGING YOUR DECISION-MAKING EFFECTIVENESS

1. The team leader should respond to the following statements (2 = strongly agree, 1 = agree, and 0 = disagree).

_____ 1. I am usually accessible to the members of my team and not hard to reach.

_____ 2. I am in close touch with the ministry and well aware of how team members feel.

_____ 3. I tend to be more concerned with the short-term performance and progress of the ministry team than with fulfillment of our long-run vision and mission.

_____ 4. I am generally very conscious of tradition and precedent when making ministry decisions.

_____ 5. I have a knack for coming up with creative alternatives to consider in decision-making.

_____ 6. I evaluate decision-making alternatives in light of ministry goals.

_____ 7. I am often too quick to compromise.

_____ 8. I am rarely caught off guard or surprised at how ministry members react to the decisions I make.

_____ 9. Many times I find it hard to stick to decisions I have made.

_____ 10. I often experience difficulties in implementing decisions.

_____ 11. Being liked is very important to me.

_____ 12. I don't mind "sticking my neck out" in making important decisions.

Score the inventory by subtracting your total for statements 3, 4, 7, 9, 10, and 11 (decision-making detractors) from your total for statements 1, 2, 5, 6, 8, and 12 (decision-making enhancers). The higher your score (on a -12 to 12 scale), the greater is your potential for making effective decisions. Compare this score with your ministry team's assessment in part 2 which follows.

2. This should be completed by members of the ministry team. They should state how much they agree (2 = strongly agree, 1 = agree, 0 = disagree) with each of the following statements about the team leader.

My team leader:

_____ 1. Is generally accessible and easy to get hold of.

_____ 2. Stays in close touch with the ministry and is aware of team member feelings.

_____ 3. Tends to be more concerned with our short-run performance than with long-run vision and mission of the
organization.
_____ 4. Is generally very conscious of tradition and precedent
when making ministry decisions.
_____ 5. Has a knack for coming up with creative alternatives to
consider in decision-making.
_____ 6. Evaluates decision-making alternatives in light of ministry goals.
_____ 7. Is often too quick to compromise.
_____ 8. Is rarely caught off guard or surprised at how team
members react to decisions.
_____ 9. Sometimes finds it difficult to stick to decisions made.
_____ 10. Often experiences difficulties in implementing decisions
once they are made.
_____ 11. Wants very much to be liked.
_____ 12. Avoids decisions involving risk.

Score the inventory by subtracting the total for statements 3, 4,
7, 9, 10, and 11 (detractors) from the total for statements 1, 2, 5,
6, 8, and 12 (enhancers). Compare this score with the leader's
own score in part 1.

● ACTION PLAN 4.2
IMPROVING DECISION-MAKING EFFECTIVENESS

Compare your assessment of your own decision-making effectiveness
(Part I of Situation Review 4.2) with the assessment of your team
members.

1. How similar are the two assessments? _____

_____

_____

_____

2. What probably accounts for any significant discrepancies in the two
profiles?

_____

_____

_____

_____

_____

3. Based on the assessments, do you feel you are an effective decision-maker?

_____

_____

_____

_____

_____

4. What appear to be your primary decision-making strengths and weaknesses?

_____

_____

_____

_____

_____

5. What can you do to improve your decision-making effectiveness?

_____

_____

_____

_____

6. How can your team help you?

_____

_____

_____

_____

_____

■ DISCUSSION MODULE 4.3
WHO DECIDES?

There's more than one way to make a decision, and the approach makes a big difference in the decision's outcome. The ministry manager can make the decision "solo," with no involvement from team members or go to the other extreme and abide by whatever the team decides on its own. Between these two poles are the options of consulting with team members individually or collectively. Which style works best depends on the circumstances surrounding the decision. *A general rule is the more team members are affected by a decision, the more they should be involved in making it.* Participation breeds commitment.

Group decision-making is also warranted when the issue is novel or complex, when creativity is needed, and when team members possess high technical expertise. Individual, or unilateral, decision-making is warranted when time is short, the matter is of a routine nature, and the ministry manager already has enough information and expertise to make the decision.

Group decision-making makes communication easier and facilitates smooth implementation of the decision. In addition, bilateral decision-making allows a greater number of alternatives to be evaluated and more information to be processed.

Group decision-making does have its drawbacks, however, since it generally takes longer and because groups can be indecisive. If the problem of "groupthink" prevails, group decision-making can prove disastrous. Team members delude themselves into believing they can do no wrong and "circle the wagons" against any form of criticism or negative feedback from those outside the group.

▲ SITUATION REVIEW 4.3
AUDIT OF SITUATIONAL DECISION-MAKING

Indicate which style of decision-making you tend to lean toward in each situation below. Choose from the following styles:

1 = You make the decision alone, with no team involvement.

2 = You ask certain team members for information about the issue (without telling them what decision you are about to make), and then make the decision on your own.

3 = You consult with team members on an individual basis about the issue involved, and then make the decision on your own.

4 = You consult with your team as a group and then make the decision on your own.

5 = You allow the team to make the decision on its own, and you agree to abide by it.

____ 1. Responding to criticism of ministry performance.

____ 2. Scheduling future ministry activities (calendar planning).

____ 3. Evaluating ministry performance and progress.

____ 4. Setting performance goals for the team as a whole.

____ 5. Setting performance goals for individual team members.

____ 6. Solving nonroutine problems.

____ 7. Defining job descriptions and team member roles.

____ 8. Developing new programs and ministry activities.

____ 9. Revising the budget.

____ 10. Evaluating team morale and motivation.

Add up your responses to all 10 items and interpret your total score as follows:

Scoring Range	Probable Interpretation
10–20	You tend to lean too heavily toward unilateral/autocratic decision-making.
21–35	You take good advantage of team wisdom and counsel in decision-making, while striving to maintain your leadership role.
36–50	You tend to go overboard on team consensus, perhaps watering down or abandoning your leadership role.

● ACTION PLAN 4.3
ACHIEVING DECISION-MAKING BALANCE

1. Have team members evaluate your responses to Situation Review 4.3. To what extent do they perceive your decision-making style the way you do?

_____

_____

_____

_____

2. According to your responses to Situation Review 4.3, do you over-rely on one of the five decision-making styles? What does your team think?

_____

_____

_____

3. If you tend to over-use unilateral decision-making or depend too heavily on the team to run itself without your leadership, explain what action steps you can take to become a more balanced decision-maker:

_____

_____

_____

_____

4. How can your team help you become a more balanced decision-maker?

_____

_____

_____

_____

■ DISCUSSION MODULE 4.4
UNDERSTANDING PROBLEM-SOLVING

Problems are not necessarily bad. When managed intelligently, problems become genuine opportunities for ministry progress, because they reveal how the ministry can be improved and strengthened. Considering how firmly entrenched the status quo is in most organizations (especially those which heavily rely on volunteers), problems serve the invaluable role of shaking things up and preventing team members from resting on their laurels.

Problems are not so much solved as they are managed or contained. Most "problems" are really symptoms of larger problems. These symptoms may be resolved in piecemeal fashion, but the larger problem doesn't evaporate. Symptoms and problems are linked together in a cause-and-effect network that resists permanent solution but can be managed.

For example, such common "people-problems" as poor communication, fluctuating morale, and tenuous cooperation are never permanently solved, because they are symptoms of the larger problem of nonoptimal teamwork—which is itself a symptom of human imperfection. Nonetheless, everyday people problems can be managed even though they are a permanent part of organizational life. Ministry leaders should therefore think of themselves as problem-managers rather than problem-solvers.

▲ SITUATION REVIEW 4.4
LOOKING FOR THE SILVER LINING

Discuss the following issues and questions with your ministry team members:

1. Identify two or three significant ministry successes over the past year:

_____

_____

_____

2. Looking at these ministry breakthroughs in retrospect, how were they linked to problems? Were the problems in any way a catalyst for ministry success?

_____

_____

_____

_____

_____

3. In retrospect, might team members have responded to these problems in a more optimistic manner, recognizing them as a "silver lining"?

_____

_____

_____

● ACTION PLAN 4.4
TURNING PROBLEMS INTO OPPORTUNITIES

Identify two or three problems your ministry team is currently wrestling with. As a team, address the following questions:
Problem:

1. What larger problem is this linked to (a symptom of)?

_____

_____

_____

2. What aspect of the ministry's status quo has this problem disrupted?

_____

_____

_____

3. In what respects can the status quo be improved upon?

_____

_____

_____

_____

_____

4. How can this problem be contained (neutralized) in the short-run?

_____

_____

_____

_____

_____

5. In what significant ways will the ministry benefit when the problem is eventually solved?

_____

_____

_____

_____

_____

6. What can you do today to keep this problem (symptom) from repeating itself in the future?

_____

_____

_____

_____

_____

7. What can be done in the future to help the team respond more
cheerfully to problems, recognizing them as a catalyst for ministry
success?

_____

_____

_____

_____

_____

■ DISCUSSION MODULE 4.5
STRATEGIES FOR PROBLEM-SOLVING

Formal problems (those involving the way the organization operates
"on paper," such as systems and procedures, policies, rules, budgets,
and written job descriptions) are often best addressed through informal means (discretionary behaviors of team members, such as friend-
ships and unstated expectations about how work is done). Likewise,
informal problems (cliques, members who let the team down, and poor
attitudes) are often best addressed through formal means (committees, written systems and procedures, and policy and goal statements). By counterbalancing *formal* and *informal* processes in this
manner, managers can compensate for imperfections (gaps) in the way
ministry activities are designed or implemented.

Consider the common example of a committee (formal structure)
hobbled by internal squabbling and inadequate leadership (informal activities). Rather than rewriting the committee's bylaws or adopting
different rules of order (formal problem-solving methods), the problem
of disharmony would probably be best handled through informal means
such as greater spontaneous fellowship among quarreling members
(e.g., meals together, off-hours recreational events, attendance of
continuing education seminars together). Poor performance of a formal
part of the organization (the committee) is bolstered by excellent per-

formance in the informal part of the organization.

Also consider the (informal) problem of team members who spend too much time socializing and "goofing off" during the work day. Rather than addressing this informal problem in an informal way (such as encouraging people to work harder), formal means will probably prove more fruitful, such as adopting a management by objectives system or increasing the frequency of meaningful on-the-record job evaluation sessions.

▲ SITUATION REVIEW 4.5
REVIEW OF PROBLEM-SOLVING TACTICS

1. Check which of the following formalized potential problem-solvers are regularly used by your team:
    ____ Written systems and procedures for doing work.
    ____ Written job descriptions.
    ____ Permanent committees.
    ____ Organization chart.
    ____ Temporary committees.
    ____ Time cards.
    ____ Written goals and plans.
    ____ Job rotation.
    ____ Written grievance system.
    ____ Management by objectives.
    ____ Periodic performance evaluation.
    ____ Brainstorming sessions.
    ____ Budgets.

2. Check which of these informal problem-solving processes are regularly used by your team:
    ____ After hours socializing and recreation.
    ____ Working meals.
    ____ "Management by walking around."
    ____ Seeking the cooperation of informal work team leaders.
    ____ Coffee break conversations.
    ____ Soliciting "off-the-record" work-related feedback one-on-one.

● ACTION PLAN 4.5
INTEGRATED PROBLEM-SOLVING

1. Based on Situation Review 4.5, does your team appear to favor formal or informal approaches to problem-solving?

_____

_____

_____

2. Which of the above formal sources are you perhaps relying on too
heavily?

_____

_____

_____

_____

3. Which informal sources are you over-relying on?

_____

_____

_____

_____

4. In the provided space, indicate formal problems you hope to address more effectively through informal means:

A. Formal problem: _____

_____

   Informal management: _____

_____

B. Formal problem: _____

_____

   Informal management: _____

C. Formal problem: _____

_____

Informal management: _____

_____

5. Now indicate how you hope to address informal problems formally:

A. Informal problem: _____

_____

Formal management: _____

_____

B. Informal problem: _____

_____

Formal management: _____

_____

C. Informal problem: _____

_____

Formal management: _____

RESOURCES FOR
DECISION-MAKING AND PROBLEM SOLVING

Allred, Thurman W. *Basic Small Church Administration*. Nashville: Convention Press, 1981.

Callahan, Kennon L. *Twelve Keys to an Effective Church*. San Francisco: Harper and Row, 1983.

Engstrom, Ted W. *Your Gift of Administration*. Nashville: Thomas Nelson Publishers, 1983.

Engstrom, Ted W., and Dayton, Edward R. *60-Second Management Guide*. Waco, Texas: Word Inc., 1984.

Lindgren, Alvin J., and Shawchuck, Norman. *Mangement for Your Church*. Indianapolis: Organization Resources Press, 1984.

Morgan, John S., and Philip, J.R. *You Can't Manage Alone*. Grand Rapids: Zondervan Publishing House, 1985.

Rush, Myron. *Management: A Biblical Approach*. Wheaton, Ill.: Victor Books, 1983.

Williams, George M. *Improving Parish Mangement*. Mystic Conn: Twenty-Third Publications, 1983.

MEDITATIONS FOR LEADERSHIP

But the greatest among you shall be your servant. And whoever exalts himself shall be humbled; and whoever humbles himself shall be exalted (Matthew 23:11-12).

But God has chosen the foolish things of the world to shame the wise, and God has chosen the weak things of the world to shame the things which are strong. That, just as it is written, "Let him who boasts, boast in the Lord" (1 Corinthians 1:27, 31).

According to the grace of God which was given to me, as a wise master builder I laid a foundation, and another is building upon it. But let each man be careful how he builds upon it. For no man can lay a foundation other than the one which is laid, which is Jesus Christ (1 Corinthians 3:10-11).

Do nothing from selfishness or empty conceit, but with humility of mind let each of you regard one another as more important than himself (Philippians 2:3).

Chapter 5

Resources for Leadership

■ DISCUSSION MODULE 5.1
THE ESSENCE OF CHRISTIAN LEADERSHIP

Christian leadership resides in the person more than the process. Ultimately Christ was a leader not because of what He did, but because of who He was. This principle is found throughout Scripture. People such as Moses, David, and Paul led because of their relationship to God, not because they were expert managers. Once we are the kinds of people God wants us to be, He will uphold us as leaders.

Christian leadership is thus a matter of personal spiritual maturity and growth. Sheep follow the shepherd not so much because he knows where green pastures are, but because they trust him and recognize his voice. Mastery of managerial skills will enhance a leader's success but is no substitute for spiritual maturity.

Christians are attracted to spiritually mature people and responsive to their influence. These salt and light team members emerge naturally as role models. They lead because they follow God! Those whom God calls to leadership He first calls to spiritual maturity.

Leaders work more through influence (role-modeling) than power (formal authority). People follow them because they want to, not because they have to. Therefore, leadership is not tied only to positions of formal authority—it is not job specific.

Since Christ's model of leadership is based on sacrificial service to others, Christian leaders expect to serve rather than to be served. This requires that we subordinate our own needs and attend to the needs of others, following Christ's example. Such selfless devotion to others is possible only for those who have enough spiritual maturity to rise above their own needs. Such leaders are able to build themselves into others because of the overflow of their spiritual blessings. Those who have the most, serve the most.

▲ SITUATION REVIEW 5.1
SALT AND LIGHT REVIEW

State how much you agree with the following statements (2 = strongly agree; 1 = agree; 0 = disagree).

_____ 1. I have several strong personal needs I depend on my ministry team to satisfy.

_____ 2. I am a positive spiritual influence on the members of my ministry team.

_____ 3. I interact with my team members primarily on a professional level and not so much on a personal level.

_____ 4. I regularly pray with the members of my ministry team.

_____ 5. I rely on my formal authority (position power) to make most things happen in the ministry.

_____ 6. I feel responsible for nurturing the growth of my team members spiritually as well as professionally.

_____ 7. I value my team members primarily for the contributions they make to the ministry.

_____ 8. Ministry team members often come to me for advice and counsel.

_____ 9. I spend about the same amount of time with each of my team members.

_____ 10. I have a strong sense of conviction that God is supporting me and the ministry work I do.

_____ 11. People don't always listen to what I have to say or follow my advice.

_____ 12. I view my work more as a ministry to serve God than as a profession that enables me to make a living.

Subtract your total for the odd-numbered statements (poor leadership practices) from your total for the even-numbered (positive leadership practices). If the difference is much below 5 or 6, you may want to prayerfully consider ways to further develop your qualities of spiritual leadership. Action Plan 5.1 will be of help to you.

● **ACTION PLAN 5.1**
EXTENDING YOUR STAKES

1. How can you take greater advantage of the following ways to build yourself into *team members:*

A. Prayer:

_____

_____

_____

_____

_____

B. Bible Study:

_____

_____

_____

_____

_____

C. Socializing and fellowship:

_____

_____

_____

_____

_____

D. Delegation:

_____

_____

_____

_____

_____

E. Recreational activities:

_____

_____

_____

_____

_____

F. "Management by walking around:"

_____

_____

_____

_____

_____

2. Consider some practical ways in which you can take greater advantage of the following to promote your own personal spiritual growth and maturity:

A. **Prayer:**

_____

_____

_____

_____

_____

B. **Bible study:**

_____

_____

_____

_____

_____

C. **Leisure time:**

_____

_____

_____

_____

_____

D. Counseling with others:

_____

_____

_____

_____

_____

E. Self-discipline and denial:

_____

_____

_____

_____

_____

_____

F. Stewardship:

_____

_____

_____

_____

_____

_____

G. **Entering into a spiritual accountability relationship with another:**

_____

_____

_____

_____

_____

3. Think about and describe how you can become a better role model in the following areas:

A. **Having time for others:**

_____

_____

_____

_____

_____

B. **Listening to others:**

_____

_____

_____

_____

_____

C. **Encouraging others:**

_____

_____

_____

_____

_____

D. Confronting others:

_____

_____

_____

_____

_____

E. Bearing patiently with others:

_____

_____

_____

_____

_____

F. Forgiving others:

_____

_____

_____

_____

_____

G. **Being receptive to the positive influence of others:**

_____

_____

_____

_____

_____

■ DISCUSSION MODULE 5.2
LEADERSHIP VISION

Leaders have a vision for transforming and renewing people through ministry. Their desire is to change the world through changing people, and they have both the zeal and patience to usher change into existence.

The transforming quality of Christian leadership resides in the leader's commitment to discipling members of the ministry team through prayer, Bible study, and being yoked together in serving capacities. The more team members grow spiritually, the more they can be transformed by the Holy Spirit.

Good leadership also serves to renew people by reminding them of ministry mission and goals, by helping restore frayed or fractured team relationships, and by enabling them to develop professionally. Good leaders invigorate team members, refresh them, and recharge their serving capacities.

Christian leaders are distinguished more by their spirituality than their managerial competence. All the administrative brilliance in the world won't transform and renew people; this is the role of the Holy Spirit.

Mature leaders seek spiritual ends using spiritual means because they have a spiritual vision. They avoid the common trap of putting their professional lives into a different "compartment" than their spiritual lives. Christ has lordship over everything the ministry leader does, including the development of professional vision.

▲ SITUATION REVIEW 5.2
ASSESSING YOUR LEADERSHIP ORIENTATION

For each number below, check whether item A or item B more accurately characterizes your tendency as a leader.

____ 1A. My desire is to serve.
____ B. My desire is to be served.
____ 2A. I focus on people.
____ B. I focus on programs and productivity.
____ 3A. I rely on God's power and enablement.
____ B. I rely on my managerial ability and human strength.
____ 4A. I accept people before I try to change them.
____ B. I try to change people before I accept them.
____ 5A. I desire to work with others.
____ B. I desire to work over others.
____ 6A. I rely on the Holy Spirit to motivate people.
____ B. I try to motivate people.
____ 7A. This is God's ministry.
____ B. This is my ministry.
____ 8A. I minister to the members of my ministry.
____ B. I manage the members of my ministry.

Check through your eight choices above. Subtract the number of B responses you checked from the number of A responses. The higher your final score, the more you probably exhibit qualities of servant leadership in your ministry.

● ACTION PLAN 5.2
STRENGTHENING SERVANT LEADERSHIP

1. Consider the scope of the constituency that you serve. In what specific ways would you like to see the people associated with your ministry (serving in the ministry and served by the ministry) transformed?

_____

_____

_____

_____

_____

2. In what ways would you like those associated with the ministry to be renewed?

_____

_____

_____

_____

_____

3. Think about the relationships you have with team members. In what ways can you better yoke yourself in a serving capacity with members of your ministry team?

_____

_____

_____

_____

_____

4. What actions can you take to invigorate the serving capacity of your team members?

_____

_____

_____

_____

_____

5. What can you do to refresh and recharge your own serving capacities?

_____

_____

_____

_____

_____

6. List the three most important goals of your ministry:

A. _____

_____

B. _____

_____

C. _____

_____

7. List the spiritual purpose, or vision of each of the ministry goals listed in question 6.

Spiritual purpose of goal A:

Spiritual purpose of goal B:

Spiritual purpose of goal C:

8. What is God trying to accomplish through your ministry team?

_____

_____

_____

_____

_____

9. What is God trying to accomplish through you?

_____

_____

_____

_____

_____

10. What is God trying to accomplish in you?

_____

_____

_____

_____

_____

■ DISCUSSION MODULE 5.3
BODY-BASED LEADERSHIP

It is easy to appreciate why leadership is portrayed as shepherding in the Bible. Like shepherds, Christian leaders must guard the flock: provide direction, overcome obstacles, protect the welfare of the body, and maintain unity. In short, Christian leaders must care for the needs of the body.

Shepherds have to be gentle, patient, and caring toward the flock, but also willing to shear the recalcitrant ewe, dispossess diseased lambs from their mothers, and separate butting rams. There is both a soft side and hard side to the job. So it is with ministry leadership. Team members must be encouraged, rewarded, and extended second chances, but they must also be challenged, stretched, and occasionally admonished.

Body-based leaders willingly shoulder both the soft and hard duties of caring for the ministry team. They strive to do what is best in God's eyes—what maximizes the serving capacity of the ministry. Body-based leadership is committed to three essential principles: (1) serving people's needs rather than their wants; (2) pruning unfruitful aspects of the ministry; (3) doing what is best for the long run rather than the short run.

Body-based leaders never lose sight of the ministry's spiritual purpose and mission and are therefore unwilling to settle for second-best (man's way instead of God's way). They strive to stay in touch with God's will through prayer; claim God's promises in Scripture; and respect God's moral laws. The Christian leader's ultimate purpose is to glorify God despite human imperfection. It is this willingness to serve and glorify God that qualifies people to serve as shepherding leaders.

▲ SITUATION REVIEW 5.3
SHEPHERDING NEEDS ASSESSMENT

1. In what three ways or areas does your ministry team most need leadership direction and guidance?

   A. _____

   _____

   B. _____

   _____

   C. _____

   _____

2. Reflect on your day-to-day service activities. What are the three greatest obstacles your team must regularly overcome in implementing the ministry?

   A. _____

   _____

   B. _____

_____

C. _____

_____

3. What three processes or activities do you most rely on to maintain team unity and cohesiveness?

A. _____

_____

B. _____

_____

C. _____

_____

4. What are the three greatest needs of your ministry team?

A. _____

_____

B. _____

_____

C. _____

_____

5. What nonessential wants are commonly mentioned by team members?

_____

_____

_____

_____

_____

6. Rank the team wants listed in question 5 in order of importance—which are most worthy of pursuing (once needs have been satisfied) and which are least worthwhile?

_____

_____

_____

_____

_____

7. What are the "soft" (supportive and affirming) ways in which you most commonly shepherd team members?

_____

_____

_____

_____

_____

8. What are the "hard" (challenging and confronting) aspects of the way you shepherd your team?

_____

_____

_____

_____

_____

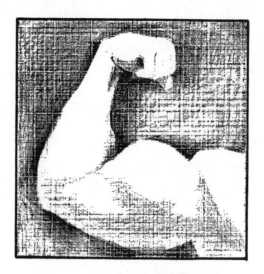

● ACTION PLAN 5.3
BODY BUILDING

1. What aspects of your ministry are currently most in need of "pruning" (changing, improving, eliminating, and strengthening)?

_____

_____

_____

_____

_____

2. What sacrifices should your ministry team be making in the short run to strengthen the ministry over the long run?

_____

_____

_____

_____

3. Which members of your team are most capable of helping you shepherd the team?

_____

_____

_____

_____

_____

4. In what ways do you need shepherding? Who is available to minister to you in these areas?

_____

_____

_____

_____

_____

5. In what specific ways do you most want to improve in "soft" shepherding skills and in "hard" skills? How can you go about implementing these changes?

_____

_____

_____

_____

_____

_____

6. Differentiate between your own needs as a ministry shepherd and your own wants:

_____

_____

_____

_____

■ DISCUSSION MODULE 5.4
MANAGING LIKE A LEADER

Thus far in chapter 5 we have discussed the character of the Christian leader: servant, role model, visionary, and shepherd. There is also a managerial side to leadership, consisting of learned behaviors that enable the leader to achieve in a team context. God prepares us as leaders not only by building our spiritual characters, but also by developing our managerial expertise. God graciously provides His leaders with tailor-made experiences that nurture spiritual and managerial maturity.

Spiritual leaders have three essential management responsibilities: (1) to build positive team attitudes; (2) to create positive expectations about team performance; and (3) to respond positively to team member behavior. These are explained in the next Situation Review and Action Plan.

▲ SITUATION REVIEW 5.4
ASSESSING YOUR MANAGERIAL SKILLS AS A
LEADER

State how much you agree with each of the following statements (2 = strongly agree, 1 = agree, and 0 = disagree).

BUILDING POSITIVE ATTITUDES
_____ 1. I recognize team member success as well as failure.
_____ 2. I expect the best and determine how to improve less than the best.
_____ 3. I praise and compliment team members for a job well done.
_____ 4. I criticize constructively rather than destructively.

_____ 5. I emphasize team member potential more than limitations.

CREATING POSITIVE EXPECTATIONS

_____ 6. I respond to all of a team member's job behavior, effective and ineffective.

_____ 7. I treat all team members fairly and equitably.

_____ 8. I announce in advance how others will benefit when our team performs its job well.

_____ 9. I accent the positive in interacting with my team.

_____ 10. I always deliver on promises.

_____ 11. I clearly communicate performance standards.

RESPONDING POSITIVELY TO BEHAVIOR

_____ 12. I strive to praise team members for what they have accomplished and to confront them over what they haven't accomplished.

_____ 13. I strive never to be neutral in how I respond to job performance.

_____ 14. I always find something to praise a team member for, even when performance success has not been fully attained.

_____ 15. I always look for ways to tap more of my team's productive potential.

Total up your responses to all fifteen positive leadership practices. The higher your score (0-30 scale), the better you are probably performing your three primary managerial responsibilities as a leader.

● ACTION PLAN 5.4
BECOMING A BETTER LEADER/MANAGER

1. Which team members probably can use a little more encouragement and positive reinforcement?

_____

_____

_____

_____

2. Which team members are in need of being challenged and stretched?

_____

_____

_____

_____

_____

3. Picture yourself as an improving leader/manager. In what respects can you develop and strengthen your capacity to encourage and to lovingly confront?

_____

_____

_____

_____

_____

4. What actions can you take to raise the performance expectations of your team?

a. _____   d. _____

b. _____   e. _____

c. _____   f. _____

5. What untapped potential for performance excellence exists within your team?

_____

_____

_____

_____

_____

6. What untapped leadership potential do you have?

_____

_____

_____

_____

_____

7. What aspects of God's power can you and your team more deeply draw upon?

_____

_____

_____

_____

_____

RESOURCES ON LEADERSHIP

Adams, Arthur Merrihew. _Effective Leadership for Today's Church._ Philadelphia: Westminster Press, 1978.

Buchanan, Edward A. _Developing Leadership Skills._ Nashville: Convention Press, 1971.

Cromer, William R., Jr. _Introduction to Church Leadership._ Nashville: Convention Press, 1971.

Dale, Robert D. _Pastoral Leadership._ Nashville: Abingdon, 1986.

Engstrom, Ted W. _The Making of a Christian Leader._ Grand Rapids: Zondervan Publishing House, 1976.

Dobbins, Gaines S. _Learning to Lead._ Nashville: Broadman Press, 1968.

Haggai, John. *Lead On!* Waco, Texas: Word, Inc., 1986.

Hendrix, John, and Householder, Lloyd. *The Equipping of Disciples.* Nashville: Boardman Press, 1977.

Hocking, David L. *Be a Leader People Follow.* Ventura, Calif.: Regal Books, 1979.

Jones, Stephen D. *Transforming Discipleship in the Inclusive Church.* Valley Forge, Pa.: Judson Press, 1984.

Leas, Speed B. *Creative Leadership Series.* Nashville: Abingdon Press, 1982.

LePeau, Andrew T. *Paths of Leadership.* Downers Grove, Ill.: InterVarsity Press, 1983.

Mosley, Ernest E. *Leadership Profiles From Bible Personalities.* Nashville: Broadman Press, 1979.

Richards, Lawrence O., and Hoeldtke, Clyde. *A Theology of Church Leadership.* Grand Rapids: Zondervan Publishing House, 1982.

Sanders, J. Oswald. *Spiritual Leadership.* Chicago: Moody Press, 1980.

Staton, Knofel. *God's Plan for Church Leadership.* Cincinnati: Standard Publishing, 1977.

Steele, David A. *Images of Leadership and Authority for the Church.* Lanham, Md.: University Press of America, 1986.

Wee Hian, Chua. *The Making of a Leader.* Downers Grove, Ill.: InterVarsity Press, 1986.

White, John. *Excellence in Leadership.* Downers Grove, Ill.: InterVarsity Press, 1986.

Youssef, Michael. *The Leadership Style of Jesus.* Wheaton, Ill.: Victor Books, 1986.

MEDITATIONS FOR MOTIVATION AND MORALE

Make me know Thy ways, O Lord; teach me Thy paths. Lead me in Thy truth and teach me, for Thou art the God of my salvation (Psalm 25:4-5).

While we look not at the things which are seen, but at the things which are not seen; for the things which are seen are temporal, but the things which are not seen are eternal (2 Corinthians 4:18).

Brethren, I do not regard myself as having laid hold of it yet; but one thing I do: forgetting what lies behind and reaching forward to what lies ahead, I press on toward the goal for the prize of the upward call of God in Christ Jesus (Philippians 3:13-14).

Devote yourselves to prayer, keeping alert in it with an attitude of thanksgiving (Colossians 4:2).

But prove yourselves doers of the word, and not merely hearers who delude themselves (James 1:22).

Chapter 6

Resources for Motivation and Morale

■ DISCUSSION MODULE 6.1
THE WELLSPRING OF MOTIVATION

Motivation for Christian ministry resides in the Holy Spirit, who empowers team members to serve with humility and sacrifice. Christian organizations should never underestimate the pivotal, energizing role of the Holy Spirit in motivation. Without this supernatural element, efforts to motivate Christian workers (both volunteers and paid staff) will prove erratic and anemic. This is the dismal fate of many secular organizations that rely exclusively on faltering, myopic human resources to motivate employees.

The central challenge of motivation is to give people a compelling reason to work enthusiastically for the organization. Human incentives and rewards—money, status, and power—tend to promote self-serving behavior and lack staying power. No wonder so many managers in the corporate world wring their hands over how to get employees to cooperate, internalize goals, and work as a team!

When motivational efforts rely primarily on self-serving external inducements—higher pay, promotions, public recognition—managers inevitably encounter some degree of frustration and disappointment in working with others. Motivation based on the quiet internal desire to glorify God by serving others is much more likely to yield professional joy and fulfillment.

▲ SITUATION REVIEW 6.1
MINISTRY POWER SOURCE

Each member of the ministry team should complete the open-ended statements below. A team meeting can then be held to compare perspectives and complete Action Plan 6.1 that follows.

1. I became part of this ministry because:

_____

_____

_____

_____

_____

2. For me, the most fulfilling aspect of working in the ministry is:

_____

_____

_____

_____

_____

3. The greatest strengths of this ministry are:

_____

_____

_____

_____

_____

4. In my opinion, the primary reasons why others have joined this ministry team are:

_____

_____

_____

_____

_____

5. The best way to increase the motivation of my team members would be to:

_____

_____

_____

_____

_____

● ACTION PLAN 6.1
GETTING A BIGGER BATTERY

1. Judging from team member responses to Situation Review 6.1, what appear to be the driving motives of your team?

_____

_____

_____

_____

2. To what extent does your ministry appear to be running on human, rather than supernatural energy?

_____

_____

_____

_____

_____

3. Are some team members apparently more motivated than others? Why?

_____

_____

_____

_____

_____

4. Based on your insight into what motivates people to serve in the ministry, on what basis could you probably best attract new team members?

_____

_____

_____

_____

_____

_____

5. Consider how each of the following might strengthen team member motivation:

A. Group prayer:

B. Group Bible study:

C. Being together more as a team:

■ DISCUSSION MODULE 6.2
MOTIVATION IS A LIFESTYLE

Too often, people conceive of motivation as something done to another person—applying certain techniques or formulas that supposedly energize behavior. Motivation is looked upon as a "faucet" that can be turned on or off at will.

This naive "spigot" model of motivation overlooks the crucial reality of relationship-building with others. Consider how Jesus worked with His disciples. He built them up by building Himself into them. Jesus recognized their needs and aspirations and helped fulfill their potential through patient encouragement and trust. He led by example, gently yoking Himself to His followers as a fellow servant. Jesus was the master motivator because he was the master relationship builder.

The Situation Review and Action Plan which follow focus on motivation through relationship-building.

▲ SITUATION REVIEW 6.2
SHIPS PASSING IN THE NIGHT?

1. The team leader should respond to the following questions:

A. In your opinion, why do team members cooperate with you and pursue your vision?

_____

_____

B. To what extent do the members of your team know you as a
   person (personality, aspirations, special interests, etc.)?

_____

_____

C. How well do team members know you spiritually (e.g., your
   theology, spiritual gifts)?

_____

_____

_____

D. How well do you know your team members on a personal
   level?

_____

_____

_____

E. How well do you know them spiritually?

_____

_____

_____

2. These questions should be answered by ministry team members:
   A. Why do you cooperate with your team leader and pursue the
      ministry's vision?

_____

_____

_____

B. To what extent do you know your team leader personally
(e.g., hobbies, aspirations, special interests)?

_____

_____

_____

C. How well do you know your leader spiritually (e.g., theology,
spiritual gifts)?

_____

_____

_____

D. How well do you feel your leader knows you personally?

_____

_____

_____

E. How well does your leader know you spiritually?

_____

_____

_____

● **ACTION PLAN 6.2**
MUTUAL BUILDING

Team members should compare and contrast parts 1 and 2 of Situation
Review 6.2 and discuss the following questions as a group:

1. To what extent has the team leader built himself or herself into team members?

_____

_____

_____

2. Do team members seem to interact with one another on a fairly superficial level?

_____

_____

_____

3. How can team members develop a more in-depth relationship personally and spiritually?

_____

_____

_____

_____

_____

4. How can team member relationships be used to foster and fuel motivation?

_____

_____

_____

_____

_____

5. In what ways can team member relationships to God be used to fuel motivation?

_____

_____

_____

_____

_____

■ DISCUSSION MODULE 6.3
SPIRITUAL PRINCIPLES OF MOTIVATION

Much can be built on the motivational base provided by the Holy Spirit. Several spiritual principles of motivation provide ministry leaders with directional bearings for productive team management. First of all, *team members should have a clear sense of how their work benefits others.* Idealistic Christians—especially volunteers—have a strong need to make a difference in the world. They are greatly encouraged when shown how their efforts help others and advance the ministry's mission.

Secondly, *the ministry leader must discern which team members are motivated more by ends and which by means.* Some people heavily identify with the goals of the ministry—its vision and quest. They are motivated by the sense of ministry "purity" and idealism. Other team members, more conscious of how the ministry actually operates, are motivated by being in harness and implementing ministry programs. Both orientations are essential, but they call for different team roles.

The third spiritual principle is to *recognize the importance of personal accountability.* Team members must know they are accountable for their efforts not only to God, but also to one another. They must see how their individual efforts are crucial to ministry success—that the "chain" is no stronger than its weakest link. Knowing they must answer to the team is a sobering reality that motivates team members to hold up their end of the work load.

The fourth spiritual principle is so familiar it is often overlooked: *nothing motivates us more than making a voluntary sacrifice on behalf of others.* This is the very essence of being a Christian! Ministry leaders should give team members ample opportunity to serve sacrificially, which means subtly coercive tactics (appeals based on guilt, strong peer pressure, or understating the real costs of doing something) are to be avoided. People don't always need an external inducement in order to work conscientiously.

▲ SITUATION REVIEW 6.3
HOW STURDY A FOUNDATION?

1. Team members should respond to the following questions individually and then share answers in a team session:

A. Over the past year, how has the work of your ministry benefited others?

_____

_____

_____

_____

_____

B. How have you gained personally? (How does the ministry minister to you?)

_____

_____

_____

_____

_____

C. What excites you most about the goals and vision of your particular ministry?

_____

_____

_____

D. What ministry activities do you enjoy the most and find fulfilling?

_____

_____

_____

_____

_____

E. I make a difference to this ministry in the following ways:

_____

_____

_____

_____

2. State how much you agree with the following statements (2 = strongly agree, 1 = agree, and 0 = disagree).

_____ 1. I make a number of important contributions to the overall success of this ministry.

_____ 2. I feel appreciated by my team members for the work I do.

_____ 3. I know what my team expects of me.

_____ 4. I let team members know what I expect of them.

_____ 5. I know I will be lovingly confronted if I let my team down in some way.

_____ 6. I would not hesitate to lovingly confront a team member who has let the group down in some way.

_____ 7. The members of my team regularly pray together.

_____ 8. The members of my team have a spiritual, as well as working, relationship with one another.

_____ 9. We strongly depend on one another.

_____ 10. We are a support group for one another.

If many members have a total score under 10 on the inventory (which lists positive motivational factors), more attention should be devoted to mutual accountability. Action Plan 6.3 will assist you.

● ACTION PLAN 6.3
BUILDING A STURDY FOUNDATION

1. The following group-oriented questions can be profitably used in focusing and guiding the team's discussion of Part 1 of Situation Review 6.3:

   A. To what extent does your team seem to be motivated by the joy of serving others?

   _____

   _____

   _____

   _____

   _____

   B. Look at your team as a whole. Which team members seem to be focused more on the ends (vision and goals) of the ministry than the means?

   _____

   _____

   _____

   _____

   C. Which members are focused more on ministry means (implementation activities) than ends?

   _____

   _____

   _____

   _____

   _____

D. How can the two types of people in questions 2 and 3 better motivate one another?

_____

_____

_____

_____

E. What is the unique niche and contribution of each team member?

_____

_____

_____

_____

_____

F. Do some team members appear to be more excited about the ministry than others? Why?

_____

_____

_____

_____

_____

2. Use the following questions to guide the team's discussion of Situation Review, part 2.
   A. In what primary ways are team members accountable to one another for the work they perform?

_____

_____

_____

_____

_____

B. How are team members spiritually accountable to one another
in your ministry?

_____

_____

_____

_____

C. In what specific, feasible ways can team accountability be
improved?

_____

_____

_____

_____

D. Where is accountability likely to break down on the team?
Why?

_____

_____

_____

_____

_____

_____

_____

E. How can mutual appreciation be improved on the team?

_____

_____

_____

_____

F. How can team members clarify what they expect of one another?

_____

_____

_____

_____

G. How strong is mutual dependency on the team? How can it be strengthened?

_____

_____

_____

_____

_____

_____

H. Are there any critical "weak links" on the team? If so, what
supportive action should be taken?

_____

_____

_____

_____

_____

■ DISCUSSION MODULE 6.4
MINISTRY MORALE

Morale (the motivational level of the overall team) is a lot like good
weather—we don't appreciate it until it's gone! And like the weather,
morale is subject to rapid change. Both commissions and omissions
can be at fault.

Ministry managers unintentionally damage team morale through
several common commissions, such as failing to keep team members
well-informed of changes that affect them or failing to consult them on
key decisions. Overly-isolated ministry leaders often dampen morale,
as do leaders who manage bureaucratically through impersonal and
inflexible procedures. Other common commissions include creating
false expectations that are not sustained (budget requests that go
unfinanced, exaggerated promises of growth and success in the ministry), and managing the organization in a competitive way such that one
ministry team "wins" (gets what it wants) only when another "loses"
(foregoes its agenda).

Ministry leaders can also damage morale through omissions—what
they fail to do. For example, managers sometimes fail to intervene
when one or more team members hamper ministry efforts with unproductive work habits (such as lack of follow through). Should the leader
fail to act in such situations, team members are apt to harbor resentment or become cynical. Similarly, when the leader is lax in praising
team members, morale will sag. This is true—and perhaps especially
so—even of idealistic Christian staff and volunteers, who many erro-

neously assume don't need "stroking."

Healthy team morale (further discussed in the next chapter) requires daily maintenance. It is easier lost than gained and subject to unpredictable swings even in the healthiest of ministries. Nevertheless, much can be done by the discerning ministry leader to maintain positive morale. Four important principles apply:

1. *Principle of visibility:* Morale is strengthened the more frequently team members see one another and expand their awareness of ministry current events. (Familiarity breeds appreciation, not contempt!)

2. *Principle of interaction:* Working together and sharing common pursuits builds morale.

3. *The niche principle.* Morale improves as each team member finds a unique niche on the team. These niches help people feel appreciated and needed.

4. *Principle of mutual sacrifice.* Team members who sacrifice together grow together. The resulting team closeness boosts morale.

▲ SITUATION REVIEW 6.4
MORALE AUDIT

Team members should state how much they agree with the following statements (2 = strongly agree, 1 = agree, 0 = disagree).

_____ 1. The morale of my team fluctuates frequently.

_____ 2. Communication between team members is not as strong as it should be.

_____ 3. Our team leader does not consult team members often enough about decisions and other administrative actions.

_____ 4. Our team leader is often inaccessible and isolated.

_____ 5. The team leader tends to relate to us more as a group than as individuals.

_____ 6. My team leader has a tendency to leave activities "hanging," without adequate follow-through or closure.

_____ 7. Our team sometimes "bites off more than it can chew" and falls short of the mark in its performance.

_____ 8. There is a sense of rivalry or "turf-protection" between ministries in this organization in such areas as budget allocations and calendar planning.

_____ 9. My team leader is sometimes too "soft" on individuals and hesitant to confront them when necessary.

_____ 10. The team leader does not always recognize member contributions and achievements.

_____ 11. The members of my team don't interact as often as they should.

___ 12. Members of my team work alone more often than together.
___ 13. The unique role occupied by each team member is not very clear.
___ 14. We don't make enough sacrifices as a team.
___ 15. I don't always look forward to the work I do on the team.

If many team members have total scores above the 7–10 range on the inventory (which consists entirely of morale-damaging factors), morale-building activities are probably needed, as will be discussed in Action Plan 6.4.

1. Based on responses to Situation Review 6.4, how strong does your team's morale appear to be?

_____

_____

_____

_____

_____

2. Are only certain members of the team experiencing morale problems? If so, why?

_____

_____

_____

_____

_____

● ACTION PLAN 6.4
CHARGING THE BATTERY

1. Seven approaches to improving team morale are listed below. Rank them in order of their potential usefulness to your team. Rank the item of greatest potential usefulness as 1, the second-to-most-useful item as 2, etc.

Rank	Morale Improver
____	Greater interaction of team members with one another.
____	Greater interaction between team leader and members.
____	Greater accessibility of the team leader.
____	Better follow-through and closure on team activities.
____	Creation of "niche" roles for team members.
____	Greater communication and cooperation with other ministry teams.
____	Greater use of praise and encouragement by the team leader.

2. Answer the following questions for the potential moral improvers ranked 1, 2, and 3 above.

A. When will your team have its first opportunity to utilize this moral improver?

_____

_____

B. Which members will benefit most from this activity?

_____

_____

C. How long do you expect it will take for team morale to measurably improve once this activity is initiated?

_____

_____

D. What specific signs will you look for to gauge how well the morale-improver is working?

_____

_____

RESOURCES ON
MOTIVATION AND MORALE

Bolt, Martin; Myers, David G. *The Human Connection*. Downers Grove, Ill.: InterVarsity Press, 1984.

Cook, William H. *Success, Motivation, and the Scriptures*. Nashville: Broadman Press, 1974.

Douglass, Stephen; Cook, Bruce; Hendricks, Howard. *The Ministry of Management*. Arrowhead Springs, San Bernardino, Calif.: Here's Life Publishers, 1981.

Eims, Leroy. *Be A Motivated Leader*. Wheaton, Ill.: Victor Books, 1982.

Jackson, Neil E., Jr. *Motivational Ideas for Changing Lives*. Nashville: Broadman Press, 1982.

Johnson, Douglas W. *Creative Leadership Series*. Nashville: Abingdon Press, 1982.

Stevens, R. Paul. *Liberating the Laity*. Downers Grove, Ill.: InterVarsity Press, 1985.

Wilson, Marlene. *How to Mobilize Church Volunteers*. Minneapolis: Augsburg Publishing House, 1983.

White, Robert N. *Managing Today's Church*. Valley Forge, Pa.: Judson Press, 1981.

MEDITATIONS FOR TEAMWORK

And be subject to one another in the fear of Christ (Ephesians 5:21).

Bearing with one another, and forgiving each other, whoever has a complaint against any one; just as the Lord forgave you, so also should you. And beyond all these things put on love, which is the perfect bond of unity (Colossians 3:13-14).

According to the grace of God which was given to me, as a wise master builder I laid a foundation, and another is building upon it. But let each man be careful how he builds upon it. For no man can lay a foundation other than the one which is laid, which is Jesus Christ (1 Corinthians 3:10-11).

Now we who are strong ought to bear the weaknesses of those without strength and not just please ourselves. Let each of us please his neighbor for his good, to his edification (Romans 15:1-2).

Therefore encourage one another, and build up one another, just as you also are doing (1 Thessalonians 5:11).

Chapter 7

Resources for Teamwork and Interpersonal Relations

■ DISCUSSION MODULE 7.1
GROWING TEAMWORK

Any experienced gardener knows that the key to a good crop is fertile soil. Prepare the soil well and Mother Nature will do her part. So it is with teamwork—create a fertile organizational climate and teamwork will follow.

Perhaps the hardest thing for many ministry managers to realize is that teamwork can't be forced to happen, any more than a garden can be forced to grow. Teamwork is the by-product of a healthy, well-managed organization where employees work cooperatively toward achieving ministry goals. These fertile conditions enable teamwork to "happen."

Gardeners foster fertile growing conditions through cultivating and fertilizing the soil, watering and weeding—and waiting patiently. Ministry leaders can also do much to cultivate fertile circumstances for teamwork. Four interpersonal processes are crucial: interaction, influence, self-control, and trust.

The first "seed" of teamwork is *interaction*. Interacting on and off the job, team members get to know one another and share common agendas: feelings, aspirations, frustrations, problems, and so forth.

When team members have something in common, they are usually open to team influence in such crucial areas as goal-setting, maintenance of high standards, and performance evaluation. *Openness to influence* is a second seed of fertile teamwork.

The third seed to germinate is that of *self-control*. In submitting to the group's influence, team members will eventually internalize ministry goals, making them their own. This reduces the need to control behavior through external means (rules, budgets, time clocks, procedures), because team members control themselves.

The teamwork cycle is completed with a fourth seed, that of *trust*. People who fall in step with the team, exercising self-control on behalf of their colleagues, quickly develop trust for one another. They act in mutually supportive ways and forge group cohesiveness.

The team leader serves as the catalyst for this four-stage cycle of teamwork, promoting interaction and consensus, encouraging commitment, and building bridges of rapport. Situation Review 7.1 and Action Plan 7.1 provide concrete suggestions for action.

▲ SITUATION REVIEW 7.1
HOW FERTILE IS YOUR GARDEN?

1. On an individual basis, team members should state how much they agree (2 = strongly agree, 1 = agree, 0 = disagree) with the following statements:

_____ 1. The members of my team interact frequently on-the-job.

_____ 2. We interact frequently off-the-job.

_____ 3. We interact productively.

_____ 4. We interact harmoniously.

_____ 5. We share our feelings openly and honestly.

_____ 6. We generally find it easy to reach consensus.

_____ 7. Few hidden agendas (secrets, undisclosed feelings, disguised motives) exist on my team.

_____ 8. The members of my team have a lot in common.

_____ 9. My team is cohesive and unified.

_____ 10. We know what we're trying to accomplish.

_____ 11. We agree on how to accomplish things.

_____ 12. I am willing to be influenced by other members of my team.

_____ 13. They are open to my influence.

_____ 14. Members of my team cooperate with one another more than they compete against each other.

_____ 15. I have strongly internalized the goals of my team (made them my own goals).

_____ 16. Team members are strongly committed to our goals.

_____ 17. Team members are strongly self-motivated to achieve goals.

_____ 18. We rarely mistrust one another's motives or intentions.

_____ 19. Team members work hard with little external pressure or direction.

_____ 20. I strongly identify with membership on my team.

2. The following questions based on Part 1 should be answered by the _ministry team as a group._

    A. Are you interacting with team members regularly and supportively? Check one: yes _____ no _____

    B. How well do you know one another, both professionally and personally?

_____

_____

_____

    C. To what extent are you open and honest with one another?

_____

_____

_____

    D. To what extent is it a struggle for team members to work together cooperatively and enthusiastically?

_____

_____

_____

E. Do you tend to do things by mutual consensus or begrudging compromise?

F. To what extent does each member of your ministry appear to be well-integrated onto the team (aware of and supportive of team goals)?

_____

_____

_____

G. To what extent have members voluntarily subordinated themselves to the group and its influence?

_____

_____

_____

H. To what extent do team members compete against each other?

_____

_____

_____

I. How strongly do team members appear to trust one another?

_____

_____

_____

_____

J. How strong is team member self-control?

_____

_____

_____

● ACTION PLAN 7.1
TILLING THE SOIL

Have the team discuss how the following might be used to generate greater teamwork and a more fertile climate for teamwork:

1. Annual planning retreats:

2. Off-the-job recreation:

3. Weekly meal together:

4. Weekly prayer session:

5. More frequent business meetings:

6. Brainstorming sessions:

7. Interaction and "cross-pollination" with other teams:

■ DISCUSSION MODULE 7.2
TEAM HEALTH

Health is much more than the absence of sickness, especially in teamwork! Healthy teamwork accomplishes more than merely getting people to work together. It produces synergy: accomplishment beyond the sum of individual team member contributions. Teamwork enables people to achieve the extraordinary through cooperation.

Team health is gauged by the team's capacity to: (1) set and internalize goals; (2) make decisions; (3) implement decisions; (4) resolve conflict; (5) change; (6) maintain accountability; and (7) satisfy team members.

When the team vision excites members, they readily "buy" into ministry goals. Decision-making consensus is readily reached because the goals are so strongly shared, which in turn facilitates smooth implementation of the decision.

Because trust runs high on healthy teams, conflict is easily resolved. Members want what's best for the team, so they respond positively to change, seeing it as an opportunity for progress. Because the team is open to change, it is accountable to other ministry groups which may see the need for and benefits of change.

Healthy teams also have satisfied members, who rely on one another for a sense of uniqueness, belongingness, fellowship, and accomplishment. Membership on the team should help each member feel, "I'm needed," "I'm unique," "I'm productive," and "I'm appreciated."

These seven ingredients of team health generally move in unison, either undergirding teamwork or unraveling it. This explains why team health rarely stagnates—it tends to improve or deteriorate over time. The factors of team health or atrophy are thus mutually reinforcing. The strong teams get stronger and the weak teams get weaker. The following Situation Review and Action Plan will help the team leader build positive team momentum.

▲ SITUATION REVIEW 7.2
TEAM HEALTH CHECK-UP

Members of the ministry team should state how strongly they agree with the statements below (2 = strongly agree, 1 = agree, and 0 = disagree).

_____ 1. Team members freely speak up about what they think.

_____ 2. We discuss decisions until a general consensus is reached.

_____ 3. New or nontraditional ideas are given a fair hearing by the team.

_____ 4. Major issues are given major time by the team.

_____ 5. Minor issues receive no more attention than they deserve.

_____ 6. We interact with mutual supportiveness and encouragement.

_____ 7. People often bring hidden (self-serving) agendas with them into team meetings.

_____ 8. The group seems afraid to change much of the time.

_____ 9. Team members more often display an attitude of independence than interdependence.

_____ 10. Initiative and responsibility are rarely shared equally by members of the team.

_____ 11. We tend to avoid issues that generate group conflict.

_____ 12. Most of our goals are "givens" and not established by group deliberation and consensus.

Score the inventory by subtracting the total for statements 7–12 (unhealthy team circumstances) from the total for statements 1–6 (healthy team circumstances). If most team members have final scores above 6, teamwork health is probably high. If most scores are below 6, or scores vary widely across the team, a "reality-orientation" meeting would probably be of benefit. Action Plan 7.2 can be used as a framework for discussion.

● ACTION PLAN 7.2
TEAM RENEWAL

How can each of the following enhance the capacity of team members to interact productively and harmoniously:

1. Better definition of team mission and goals:

_____

_____

2. Arranging agenda items for team meetings in order of importance:

_____

_____

_____

3. Listening to all the strong points of a new idea before discussing any of the drawbacks:

_____

_____

_____

4. Establishing a written list of criteria by which to evaluate team ideas and proposals:

_____

_____

_____

5. Providing team members with information before meetings to facilitate advance "homework" preparation for the meeting:

_____

_____

_____

6. Composing the minutes of team meetings around what was beneficially accomplished rather than what agenda items were discussed:

_____

_____

_____

■ DISCUSSION MODULE 7.3
TEAM-BUILDING

Team-building is an on-going process that is never really completed—healthy teams just keep on changing, maturing, and adapting. Team-building involves knowing team members, catering to them, and facilitating member interaction. The team leader must be at the helm of all three processes. Teams can't develop themselves without leadership!

The team leader must stay in close touch with member needs, wants, and idiosyncracies. Which members take initiative? Who are the talkers and the listeners? Who are the risk-takers, the dreamers, the practical traditionalists? Who is open-minded? Who lacks boldness and self-confidence?

The better the team leader knows team members as individuals, the better he or she can cater to them—utilize their capabilities, shore up weaknesses, and build the job around them. Knowing team members as unique individuals allows the team leader to treat them distinctively.

When team members know one another well and occupy a unique niche on the team, productive, harmonious interaction is easily facilitated by the leader. Nothing stimulates enthusiastic cooperation more than the sense of individual belongingness, acceptance, and uniqueness.

▲ SITUATION REVIEW 7.3
GETTING TO KNOW YOU

The following questions should be answered by the *team leader:*

1. Which team member exerts the greatest influence on the group?

2. Who is the group's peacemaker and conflict-resolver?

3. Who is the discussion catalyst?

4. Who are the most cooperative, compliant team members?

5. Which team members have a tendency to be negative, cynical, or critical?

6. Who is generally best-prepared and organized?

7. Which members are domineering and strong-willed?

8. Who is most likely to take initiative?

9. Are there any loners on the team who hesitate to interact?

10. Are they any cliques within the team? If so, who's "in" and who's "out"?

11. Who are the most objective, open-minded team members? The most biased and inflexible?

12. Who are the discussion "hogs" (dominators)?

13. Which members express their feelings and who bottles them up?

14. Which team member is most respected? Why?

15. Who do you like most on the team? Why?

● ACTION PLAN 7.3
NICHE-PICKING

1. Based on Situation Review 7.3, identify who on your team should probably occupy the following niches:
    1. Sparkplug (making things happen): _____
    2. Analyst (rational deliberator): _____
    3. Dreamer (optimistic idealist): _____
    4. Peacemaker (conflict resolver): _____
    5. Engineer (project organizer): _____

   6. Traffic cop (project controller): _____
   7. Friend (developer of social interaction): _____
   8. Helper (cooperative follower): _____
   9. Maverick (nontraditionalist): _____
  10. Bridge-builder (reaching out to other teams): _____

■ DISCUSSION MODULE 7.4
TEAMWORK QUICKSAND

Teamwork is built on interpersonal relationships—the ability of people to interact productively and harmoniously. When interpersonal relationships deteriorate, so does teamwork. Team leaders must be keenly sensitive to warning signals—"handwriting on the wall"—of interpersonal problems developing on the team. The five most common warning signals are:

   1. *Poor communication:* result of the failure of team members to understand one another; focus on talking rather than listening; verbal hostility, etc.

   2. *Sloppy implementation:* "the-right-hand-doesn't-know-what-the-left-hand-is-doing" syndrome.

   3. *Avoidance:* members show a pattern of avoiding disagreement, avoiding accountability, or avoiding one another.

   4. *Chronic dissatisfaction:* occurs when certain members acquire a negative, pessimistic, or critical spirit that casts a shadow of gloom over team activities.

   5. *Loss of trust:* team members doubt one another's motives, submerge agendas, and begin to question the ministry vision.

   The five items cited above do not actually cause team problems. They are merely symptoms of the problem of poor interpersonal relations, which is itself a symptom of a deeper problem: spiritual immaturity. Spiritually immature people inevitably encounter difficulties in working together, because they often act and move out of self-interest and pride. A little bit of true Christian humility can go a long way toward correcting the problem and promoting healthy interpersonal relationships and teamwork!

   Situation Review 7.4 and Action Plan 7.4 provide helpful guidelines for building team humility.

▲ SITUATION REVIEW 7.4
AN OUNCE OF HUMILITY

Team members should answer the following questions on an individual basis:

1. In what different ways are you dependent on other members of your team?

_____

_____

_____

_____

_____

2. What strengths do other team members possess which you lack?

_____

_____

_____

_____

3. In what ways have team members helped you excel on your job in the past?

_____

_____

_____

_____

4. What team niches are filled by other members?

_____

_____

_____

_____

_____

5. Consider your role in your church or organization. How does being a team member help you make more contributions to the ministry than working independently?

_____

_____

_____

_____

_____

● **ACTION PLAN 7.4**
DEVELOPING INTERPERSONAL FINESSE

All team members, including the leader, should address how each of the following could enhance their interpersonal relationships on the team:

1. Criticizing the act, not the person:

_____

_____

_____

_____

_____

2. Giving relationships daily maintenance:

_____

_____

_____

_____

_____

3. Helping others to help themselves:

_____

_____

_____

_____

4. Striving to change oneself as the basis for changing others:

_____

_____

_____

_____

5. Listening more, talking less:

_____

_____

_____

_____

_____

6. Praying regularly for and with others about ministry matters as well as personal concerns:

_____

_____

_____

_____

_____

7. Focusing on the personal qualities of colleagues more than their productivity:

_____

_____

_____

_____

_____

RESOURCES ON TEAMWORK

Brown, Jerry, W. *Church Staff Teams That Win.* Nashville: Convention Press, 1979.

Griffin, Em. *Getting Together.* Downers Grove, Ill.: InterVarsity Press, 1982.

Johnson, Douglas W. *Creative Leadership Series.* Nashville: Abingdon Press, 1987.

Perry, Lloyd. *Getting The Church On Target.* Chicago: Moody Press, 1977.

Powers, Bruce P. *Church Administration Handbook*. Nashville: Broadman Press, 1985.

Rush, Myron. *Management: A Biblical Approach*. Wheaton, Ill.: Victor Books, 1983.

Schaller, Lyle E. *The Multiple Staff and the Larger Church*. Nashville: Abingdon Press, 1980.

Senter, Mark. *The Art of Recruiting Volunteers*. Wheaton, Ill.: Victor Books, 1983.

Wedel, Leonard E. *Church Staff Administration*. Nashville: Broadman Press, 1978.

Wilson, Marlene. *How To Mobilize Church Volunteers*. Minneapolis: Augsburg Publishing House, 1983.

MEDITATIONS FOR CONFLICT AND CHANGE

A new commandment I give to you, that you love one another, even as I have loved you, that you also love one another. By this all men will know that you are My disciples, if you have love for one another (John 13:34-35).

Now all these things are from God, who reconciled us to Himself through Christ, and gave us the ministry of reconciliation (2 Corinthians 5:18).

For He Himself is our peace, who made both groups into one, and broke down the barrier of the dividing wall (Ephesians 2:14).

And so, as those who have been chosen of God, holy and beloved, put on a heart of compassion, kindness, humility, gentleness and patience, bearing with one another, and forgiving each other, whoever has a complaint against any one; just as the Lord forgave you, so also should you. And beyond all these things put on love, which is the perfect bond of unity. And let the peace of Christ rule in your hearts, to which indeed you were called in one body; and be thankful (Colossians 3:12-15).

But the wisdom from above is first pure, then peaceable, gentle, reasonable, full of mercy and good fruits, unwavering, without hypocrisy. And the seed whose fruit is righteousness is sown in peace by those who make peace (James 3:17-18).

Chapter 8

Resources for Conflict and Change

■ DISCUSSION MODULE 8.1
CONFLICT: FRIEND OR FOE?

When imperfect people interact in imperfect ways, conflict results. Conflict is inevitable in all organizations, including those with a Christian mission. However, destructive conflict is not inevitable. Despite what many people think, conflict is not necessarily bad and shouldn't always be avoided.

Conflict can play a constructive role when it prompts members of the ministry team to clarify their goals and communicate forthrightly. Conflict can move team members to greater accomplishment through challenging them with higher standards. Conflict can heighten mutual understanding between team members and serve as a catharsis in "clearing the air." Constructive conflict can also be used to identify ministry deficiencies, overcome lethargy, and generate new solutions to old problems.

The dark side of conflict is all too familiar. Conflict is destructive and should be avoided when it siphons off valuable energy that could otherwise be spent on productive activity. Conflict is destructive when "might conquers right," and when it focuses on personalities more than issues. The telltale signs of destructive conflict range from team member frustration and aggression to noncooperation and withdrawal.

The goal of every ministry manager handling conflict should be to neutralize its destructive potential while exploiting its constructive possibilities. Since conflict won't go away, ministry leaders should endeavor to manage it effectively and make it work for them.

The first step in constructively managing conflict is to understand its root causes. These are both personal and interpersonal in nature. One primary source of interpersonal, or team, conflict is *lack of goal assimilation*. The seeds of conflict are sown whenever team members fail to internalize ministry goals and "own" them. In the absence of shared goals, team members have little basis for consensus and compromise, so essential for conflict avoidance.

The second major source of team conflict stems from *lack of "suboptimization"*—the team's unwillingness to make sacrifices on behalf of the larger organization. When team members are willing to put the organization's needs ahead of team needs, most conflicts can be defused.

The seeds of conflict, however, are more likely to be rooted in the individual than the group. Five human imperfections are particularly at fault: disobedience, independence, self-sufficiency, inflexibility, and pride.

Conflict can stem from the flawed tendency some of us have to second-guess decisions, doubt motives, or question the judgment of others in the group. Conflict may also surface over our desire to stand alone and avoid dependency relationships, even when others seek to help us. Self-sufficient people are slow to nurture other team members who are less self-reliant.

Inflexible people may unintentionally generate conflict by caring more about how something is done than the mission itself, creating low potential for constructive compromise or acquiescence. Similarly, prideful team members are sometimes the cause of conflict because of their desire for recognition. This struggle to be in charge inevitably breeds jealousy and resentment.

▲ SITUATION REVIEW 8.1
CONFLICT DIAGNOSIS

1. Team members should indicate how much they agree with the statements below (2 = strongly agree, 1 = agree, 0 = disagree).

_____ 1. Conflict is not necessarily a sin.

_____ 2. Working through conflicts in the past has strengthened the team and helped us work together better.

_____ 3. We have a tendency to avoid conflict and hope that it will go away.

_____ 4. It is not unusual for members of my team to be frustrated about one thing or another.

_____ 5. Even when members of my team disagree about something, they tend to remain supportive and cooperative.

_____ 6. I tend to psychologically withdraw from the team when conflict surfaces.

_____ 7. My team has wasted a great deal of time and energy in the past dealing with various conflicts.

_____ 8. The team leader often has to take strong action to overcome conflicts.

_____ 9. The members of my team are generally more concerned with what we're striving to accomplish than with how we will accomplish it.

_____ 10. We have learned through experience how to effectively resolve conflicts on the team.

Team members should score the inventory by subtracting the total for statements 3, 4, 6, 7, and 8 (unhealthy circumstances for conflict) from the total for statements 1, 2, 5, 9, and 10 (healthy circumstances). One a 10-point scale, the closer the subtracted score is to 10, the greater your team potential for dealing with conflict in a healthy, constructive way. If many team members end up with high scores, the more this healthy diagnosis about teamwork appears to be warranted. Action Plan 8.1 provides practical guidelines for enhancing the constructive potential of conflict.

2. Individual team members should indicate the extent each of the following has fueled team conflicts in the past (2 = a frequent source of conflict, 1 = an occasional source of conflict, and 0 = seldom or never a source of conflict).

_____ Personality clashes.

_____ Disagreement about goals or mission.

_____ Wanting to implement actions in different ways.

_____ Infrequent communication and interaction.

_____ Failure of team members to internalize goals.

_____ Unwillingness to sacrifice on behalf of the larger organization.

_____ Selfishness.

_____ Second-guessing team member actions.

____ Independent, maverick spirit.
____ Inflexible, close-mindedness.
____ Recognition-seeking.
____ "Empire-building" (viewing the team as more important than
the overall organization).

Action Plan 8.1 provides a framework to help your team assess its conflict patterns.

● ACTION PLAN 8.1
CONSTRUCTIVE CONFLICT

1. The next time your team encounters a conflict, process through the following questions before attempting to resolve it:
   Description of the conflict:

   A. Using Part 2 of Situation Review 8.1, what is the apparent root cause of this conflict?

   _____

   B. To what extent has this conflict been caused by styles of team interaction rather than differences in goals or vision?

   _____

   _____

   _____

   C. Is the conflict based on a matter of principle that cannot be compromised or merely a matter of personal preference?

   _____

   _____

   _____

   D. How many team members are directly involved in this conflict? Is this truly a team conflict, or one between just a few personalities?

   _____

_____

_____

E. What would probably happen if this conflict were simply ignored by the team?

_____

_____

_____

F. Are any members of the team reluctant or afraid to deal with
the conflict? If so, why?

_____

_____

_____

G. Does this appear to be the best time to deal with the conflict?
If not immediately addressed, might the conflict resolve itself
with little intervention?

_____

_____

_____

H. Examine the history involved. To what extent has the conflict
stemmed from the team's failure to adequately resolve past
differences?

_____

_____

_____

_____

I. Should the team leader take any sort of unilateral action in helping to resolve the conflict? If so, what?

_____

_____

_____

_____

_____

J. In what specific ways are team members open to compromise in resolving this conflict?

_____

_____

_____

_____

_____

K. How will the overall organization benefit if the conflict is satisfactorily resolved?

_____

_____

_____

_____

_____

L. How have other ministry teams in the organization resolved similar conflicts in the past?

_____

_____

_____

_____

_____

2. As a team, discuss the *potential* of each of the following for resolving the team conflict you are addressing:

A. Clarification of ministry mission and goals:

B. Greater frequency of communication and interaction:

C. Putting ends (where we're heading) before means (how we're going to get there):

D. More frequent discussion of team mission and goals to achieve greater consensus and commitment:

E. Identifying and clarifying the needs and "agendas" of individual team members:

■ DISCUSSION MODULE 8.2
STRATEGIES FOR RESOLVING CONFLICT

Even though conflict has constructive potential, it must nonetheless be resolved. Unresolved conflict on the ministry team can become a ravaging cancer if ignored or treated with a mere "Band-Aid." A number of conflict-reduction strategies are available which can help the ministry team work "smarter" rather than harder in preventing and resolving conflict.

Underlying these conflict strategies are three cardinal rules for preventing and containing conflict damage. The first of these is that *conflict must never be permitted to engulf people and personalities rather than issues*. Person-centered conflict is always destructive, not only because of its emotion-charged nature, but also because it offers few opportunities for compromise.

The second cardinal rule for containing conflict is to *separate the feelings of people from their thoughts*. Little can be done in the short-run to change the way people feel about conflict issues. Emotions are hard to predict and contain, but thoughts are open to examination, discussion, and concession. Much can be accomplished by team members who are willing to confront issues in an open-minded way.

The third cardinal rule is to *deal with conflict in a nonconfrontational way*. Avoid a bitter "showdown" that demands instantaneous resolution of the problem "one way or the other." Confrontations push people into saying things they later regret and into making headstrong decisions. This actually fuels the fire and perpetuates the conflict in the future.

Several excellent strategies are available for coping with conflict. The most basic of these involves the effort to *formulate "superordinate" goals that transcend everyone on the ministry team*—they are bigger than any individual's goals or agenda. Superordinate goals form the very nucleus of the ministry vision and become a common cause and commitment for all teams within the organization. For Christian organizations, the superordinate goal of serving Christ is the one overarching aim of all ministry teams.

A second conflict strategy involves *breaking the conflict down into smaller issues* that the team can "get a handle" on. Called *fractionizing*, this strategy helps team members isolate the root cause of a conflict and separate symptoms from problems. Even seemingly gargantuan conflicts can be broken down into problem points or "hot spots" that are specific enough for the team to capably handle.

A third master strategy for handling conflict seeks to *stimulate greater "cross pollination" between ministries in the organization*, helping team members to better identify and "bond" with one another through common pursuits. The more people from diverse ministries interact supportively, the greater their sense of shared vision and interdependence. The potential for conflict melts as team members more fully identify and empathize with one another.

Compromise is the fourth strategy for handling conflict. This old standby does indeed hold marvelous potential for resolving conflict, but only when used under the right circumstances. Compromise is definitely not a cure-all for conflict. Compromise works when the conflict centers around means (how we'll do something) rather than ends (what our purpose is). To ask committed team members to compromise their ideals is asking for frustration and strife.

Circumstances for constructive compromise are ripe when team members are so "sold out" to ministry goals that they're willing to make implementation concessions to achieve these goals. Goal-driven team members are usually open to changes or concessions that facilitate progress. Compromise that does not jeopardize the ultimate ministry mission will actually be welcomed under these circumstances.

Situation Review 8.2 and Action Plan 8.2 provide specific guidelines for formulating and implementing conflict resolution strategies.

▲ SITUATION REVIEW 8.2
ASSESSING THE CONFLICT ENVIRONMENT

1. Identify a real or potential conflict within your ministry and analyze it using the following questions.
Conflict issue:

A. To what extent does this conflict seem to center on people and personalities rather than issues? What interpersonal frictions and tensions currently exist on the ministry team?

_____

_____

_____

_____

_____

B. Does this conflict seem to be rooted more in people's emotions or their ideas? How do you know?

_____

_____

_____

_____

_____

C. To what extent is this the result of a confrontational approach among team members? Was this confrontation really necessary and unavoidable?

_____

_____

_____

_____

D. Does your team have one or more superordinate goals that are more important to its members than personal goals? If so, what specific evidence indicates the presence of these superordinate goals?

_____

_____

_____

_____

_____

E. To what extent is this conflict really made up of smaller conflicts that have accumulated over a period of time? If the smaller conflicts were to be resolved, would the larger conflict then eventually "evaporate"?

_____

_____

_____

_____

_____

_____

F. Do you feel this conflict may be the result of lack of communication and interaction between your ministry team and others in the organization?

_____

_____

_____

_____

_____

G. Does this conflict center more on the goals and mission of your team or the way in which goals are to be pursued and implemented?

_____

_____

_____

_____

H. To what extent are members of your team open to concession and compromise that would enhance goal attainment? How can you verify this?

_____

_____

_____

_____

_____

2. Based on Situation Review 8.2, place a check in the appropriate columns below:

A. This conflict seems to center more on:
   _____ Personalities or _____ Issues
   _____ Emotions or   _____ Ideas
   _____ Confrontation or _____ Avoidance
   _____ Implementation (means) or _____ Goals (ends)
   _____ The past or _____ The future
   _____ Commissions (what the team did) or _____ Omissions
         (what the team failed to do)
   _____ Interactions of team members with themselves or
         _____ With other teams

● ACTION PLAN 8.2
RESOLVING CONFLICT STRATEGICALLY

If most of the items checked by your team in Part 2 of Situation Review 8.2 were in the left column, the nature of the conflict under review is probably "hot." A majority of checked items in the right column indicates a "cooler" type of conflict. "Hot" conflict is generally people-intensive, emotional, and based on divisive actions of the past. By contrast, "cool" conflict tends to be intellectual (issue-oriented), concerned with perceived intentions more than actual behaviors, and idealistic ("coulds" and "shoulds").

1. If the nature of your conflict seems to be of the "hot" variety, discuss the potential of the following strategies for your team:
   A. Getting conflicting team members to "bury the hatchet" (over-look their personality differences) and put the mission of the team in the forefront:

B. Minimizing the use of "I" and "me" and maximizing "we" and "us":

C. Speaking in the future tense rather than past tense:

D. Replacing "I feel" with "I think":

E. Focusing more on intentions than actual behaviors:

F. Stressing what we can accomplish in the future more than what we failed to accomplish in the past:

2. If the nature of your team conflict is more of the "cool" variety, consider the potential of the following strategies:
   A. Discussion of what actions individual team members want to take regardless of how they feel about the team mission:

   B. Emphasis on the team's rich legacy of past accomplishments and fruits of cooperation:

C. Focus on "bridges" team members have built to one another:

D. Focus on the unique and distinctive contributions of individual team members:

E. Sharing of how members have enjoyed team interactions even when goals were not ideally achieved:

■ DISCUSSION MODULE 8.3
WHY CHANGE IS EASY TO RESIST

Most people have a love-hate relationship with change. They love the opportunities it frequently affords but hate its disruptions and inescapable adjustments. This explains why change is so commonly resisted to one extent or another by us all.

The status quo is a security blanket which we are reluctant to leave behind. Change requires effort and energy and is not entirely predictable. Sometimes the benefits of change are not obvious to everyone involved, especially if they've not had a hand in initiating it. Other times a person's resistance to change is no more complicated than a simple, "What's in it for me?"

Other reasons for resisting change are not so superficial. Many fear change will expose personal inadequacies or resurrect dormant conflicts on the team. Others worry that change may disrupt team momentum or jeopardize "turf protection."

Since change is inevitable—a permanent fixture in our complex society—ministry managers must strive to use it as a tool for team progress and advancement. This calls for pragmatic strategy. Four fundamental questions underlie the ministry change strategy:

1. How will the change benefit the ministry in general and team members in particular?
2. What price must be paid to solidify the change?
3. When should the change occur?
4. What role should each team member play in the change process?

This change strategy is made operational in the following Situation Review and Action Plan.

▲ SITUATION REVIEW 8.3
HOW HIGH IS THE WALL OF RESISTANCE?

Team members should indicate how strongly they agree (2 = strongly agree, 1 = agree, 0 = disagree) with the following questions about change.

_____ 1. Things are currently going very well for our team.

_____ 2. Team members are strongly committed to what is best for the overall team.

_____ 3. The members of the team seem to enjoy discussions of how individuals are performing and the contributions they each make.

_____ 4. Past ministry changes have not always helped the team's performance.

_____ 5. Several times in the past, team members were surprised by the difficulty and challenge of bringing about a change.

_____ 6. The team has generally been able to implement changes smoothly and efficiently.

_____ 7. We stay so busy with on-going ministry activities, it is often hard to find the time to implement changes.

_____ 8. We rarely lose sight of our goals and mission.

_____ 9. Several times in the past, the team hesitated to adopt a change because we were unsure if the benefits outweighed the costs.

_____ 10. We haven't always introduced needed changes at the optimum time.

Each team member's inventory should be scored by subtracting the total for statements 4, 5, 7, 9, and 10 (unfavorable change climate factors) from the total for 1, 2, 3, 6, and 8 (favorable change climate factors). The higher the score on a 10 point scale, the more favorable the team's change climate would appear to be. Low scores, near 0, very possibly point toward a significant resistance to change on the team.

● ACTION PLAN 8.3
OVERCOMING RESISTANCE TO CHANGE

The team leader should identify a change the team will soon tackle. By discussing this change in light of the following questions, much can be done to overcome unnecessary resistance.

Change under consideration:

1. How have things been going "right" for the team recently? Where have you succeeded and excelled?

_____

_____

_____

_____

_____

2. Cite recent examples of how team members have positively responded to what was in the team's best interest:

_____

_____

_____

_____

_____

3. Cite recent examples of outstanding contributions made by individual team members:

_____

_____

_____

_____

_____

4. Identify past instances where change brought about improvements in team performance and success:

_____

_____

_____

_____

_____

5. What has your team learned about the nature of the change process from the past that will make it easier for you to implement change in the future?

_____

_____

_____

_____

_____

6. Is now the best time to introduce this change? Might it be beneficial to wait?

_____

_____

_____

_____

_____

7. How will the overall team be better off as the result of introducing this change?

_____

_____

_____

_____

_____

_____

8. How will individual team members be better off personally?

_____

_____

_____

_____

_____

■ DISCUSSION MODULE 8.4
WORKING SMARTER RATHER THAN HARDER AT CHANGE

Much of the time, we're our own worst enemy when it comes to change. We either pick the wrong time to initiate the change, undertake it for the wrong reasons, or "shoot ourselves in the foot" while implementing it.

Perhaps the first step in "smart" change is recognizing when it is needed. A number of telltale signs suggest the need for ministry change. These include creeping lethargy in the ministry, inadequate team unity or togetherness, greater frequency of brushfires, and sagging vitality of leadership. Sometimes change is needed as a catalyst to "shake-up" the ministry team; other times it serves to solidify and stabilize team accomplishment.

Change should never be undertaken, however, as a virtue in itself— change for the sake of change. Nor should it be a "knee-jerk" reaction to emotional or political pressure. Change is an energy-monopolizing, high resource process that must not be pursued frivolously.

Smart change requires good timing and a "thawed" organization climate not dominated by routine. A particularly auspicious time for change is during a natural transition in the organization, such as a changing of the guard in leadership, the start of a new budget period, or undertaking a major new challenge (e.g., building program, re-financing).

Smart change also recognizes the crucial importance of opinion-leaders in the organization. These influential people can champion the change one-on-one, insuring that colleagues are adequately informed about its benefits and costs. The battle for change is waged most successfully here in the trenches where team members interact.

Several other principles help undergird the smart change process. Significant change should not be undertaken suddenly, autocratically, or in a vacuum (in isolation from those affected by it). Political tactics, such as "divide and conquer" and "end-runs," must be steadfastly resisted, along with visions of grandeur that would try to change the entire organization all at once, rather than one manageable piece at a time. Even more importantly, change undertaken without fervent prayer will almost certainly be stillborn. In the final analysis, change is God's prerogative. The human timetable for change must be carefully synchronized with the divine schedule!

▲ SITUATION REVIEW 8.4
A TIME FOR CHANGE?

Team members should state how much they agree with the following questions (2 = strongly agree, 1 = agree, and 0 = disagree).

_____ 1. I often feel the work of this ministry is dull and routine.

_____ 2. Our source of team unity and togetherness is not as strong as it could be.

_____ 3. The team has experienced an unusual number of "brush-fires" lately.

_____ 4. The team would really benefit from a "shake-up" of some sort.

_____ 5. People outside our team in the organization are not very familiar with the activities and pursuits of our team.

_____ 6. The most influential behind-the-scenes people in the organization enthusiastically support and promote the activities and pursuits of my ministry team.

_____ 7. Our ministry is currently in a state of transition which is disrupting the status quo.

_____ 8. The members of my team spend a lot of quality time with one another in prayer.

_____ 9. Our ministry team rarely engages in independent actions isolated from the rest of the organization.

_____ 10. Our team hesitates to undertake activities that won't smoothly mesh with what other ministry teams are doing.

The responses to all ten statements (indicating a fertile change climate) should be totaled. High scores, on a 0–20 scale, indicate not only a high need for change on the team but also favorable circumstances for bringing it about. Lower scores reflect less perceived need for change and less fertile circumstances for bringing it about.

● ACTION PLAN 8.4
A FERTILE CLIMATE FOR CHANGE

The following questions will help the team and its leader create fertile conditions for the change process. An anticipated change should be evaluated in light of these action-focused questions:

Change Under Consideration:

1. Who on the team supports this change?

_____

_____

_____

2. Who outside the team in the organization supports the change?

_____

_____

_____

3. How secure are members with the current ministry status quo?

_____

_____

_____

4. Why should the team want to make this change?

_____

5. To what extent are team members merely tolerating the change?

_____

_____

_____

6. Is there a strong champion for this change on the team?

_____

_____

_____

7. What type of change is most needed on the team now: evolutionary or revolutionary?

_____

_____

_____

8. Is this the right time for the change? How do you know?

_____

_____

_____

9. To what extent does the team feel politically pressured into making the change?

_____

_____

_____

10. How high a price is the team willing to pay for the change?

_____

_____

_____

■ DISCUSSION MODULE 8.5
SUCCESSFUL CHANGE STRATEGY

Successful change is founded on basic principles that apply to a variety of situations. These principles, which are the foundation of change strategy, call for change to be discerned, communicated, legitimized, and planned.

The first step in successful change involves _getting organization members to clearly recognize_ why it is needed and how it will prove beneficial. There must be a personalized relationship between those advocating the change and those affected by it, so that common bridges of support can be built. These relationship bridges should be sturdy enough to hold up under the "traffic" of team members working with each other as the change is implemented.

The pending change, "warts and all," must be _sensitively and creatively communicated_ to all parts of the organization. Informal means of communication, such as meals shared and casual hallway conversations, should be stressed over formal means (memos, newsletters, etc.) because of the one-on-one selling opportunities afforded by personal contacts. The change should be explained to people in light of their unique personal needs and orientation, so they will enthusiastically accept the change rather than only passively tolerate it.

Legitimizing the change is the third phase. The _proposed change should be visibly endorsed by ministry leaders_ throughout the organization, "officially" discussed at formal meetings, and given ceremonial recognition (such as inclusion in the budget or the focus of attention on bulletin boards and other avenues of organizational public relations).

In the planning phase of change _strategy, people and resources must be linked together_ according to a clearly defined implementation schedule. Team members should be equipped with time, resources, and political support to make the change a concrete reality, not an abstract ideal. Information must be gathered and processed, meetings scheduled and held, and goals translated into action plans.

As the team leader navigates through the four change strategy phases, several additional realities about change should be kept in mind. First of all, it should be remembered that leaders are almost always the most change-oriented members in an organization, so they should not expect too much too soon. Unless at least three quarters of team members support a proposed change, the leader should probably back off and not press matters in the short-run. The fervent opposition of even a small minority of organization members can stymie the change program.

Change should usually be implemented in a gradual, evolutionary manner that doesn't overwhelm team members. In addition, the course of least resistance should be followed by introducing the change in the very most supportive part of the organization. An immediate positive effect greatly enhances the long run prospects of any change.

Sometimes the organization is not quite ready for change to be introduced. Under these circumstances, the leader would be smart to do a little seed planting: introduce the change idea and then patiently cultivate it over time. When the team is ready for it, someone else will invariably suggest the idea or a variation, and the leader can go to work—even if someone else gets credit for the idea. Humility has its advantages in a number of contexts!

Under no circumstances should a frustrated team leader resort to "end-run" tactics to "sneak" change by entrenched team members. The political fallout of manipulative change tactics can ruin a leader overnight. The status quo is always preferable to "open revolution in the streets."

● SITUATION REVIEW 8.5
CHANGE IN RETROSPECT

The team leader should identify a major change recently implemented by the ministry team. Those affected by the change, both inside and outside the team, should critique the change implementation process by stating how much they agree with each of the following statements (2 = strongly agree, 1 = agree, 0 = disagree).

Change under review:

_____ 1. I clearly understood the reason for this change.
_____ 2. I supported this change.
_____ 3. I am satisfied with my participation in the process of bring-ing the change about.
_____ 4. I understood the costs as well as the benefits of this change.
_____ 5. I feel the change was adequately discussed and planned.

___ 6. The change was initiated and implemented in a personal, rather than impersonal manner.

___ 7. The change was officially endorsed by the organization before being implemented.

___ 8. The change was smoothly implemented and well-coordinated.

___ 9. I was aware of the goals of the change.

___ 10. I did not feel pressured or pushed to accept the change.

___ 11. There has been no visible opposition to this change.

___ 12. The change was implemented sensitively and at a reasonable pace.

___ 13. I'm glad we made this change.

___ 14. The organization has benefited from the change.

___ 15. I would like all future changes to be handled in this same sensible manner.

The responses to all 15 statements (positive strategies for change) should be totaled. High scores on the 30-point scale reflect a well-managed change strategy. Low scores would suggest the need to work "smarter" rather than harder in initiating and implementing change. Statements that received scores of 0, reflecting disagreement, are "red flags" that signal the need for improvement.

● ACTION PLAN 8.5
CHANGE FULL SPEED AHEAD

The following questions can help the ministry leader design an effective strategy for introducing change. The questions should be addressed by the team as a whole.

Change being considered:

1. Who will be directly affected by this change?

_____

_____

2. Who will implement the change?

_____

_____

3. Who is likely to enthusiastically support the change?

_____

_____

4. Who is likely to merely tolerate the change? Why?

_____

_____

5. Is anyone likely to oppose the change? Why?

_____

_____

6. What positive actions can you take before the change process is begun to overcome problems of apathy or resistance?

_____

_____

_____

_____

7. What actions will you take to have the change officially endorsed and legitimized?

_____

_____

_____

_____

8. How will you "sell" the change within your organization? Who will do the selling?

_____

_____

_____

_____

_____

9. According to the results of Situation Review 8.5, what should you do differently in introducing future changes?

_____

_____

_____

_____

_____

_____

10. How will you evaluate whether or not the proposed change was effectively implemented?

_____

_____

_____

_____

_____

_____

RESOURCES ON CONFLICT AND CHANGE

Bolt, Martin; Myers, David G. *The Human Connection.* Downers Grove, Ill.: InterVarsity Press, 1984.

Engstrom, Ted W., and Dayton, Edward R. *60-Second Management Guide.* Waco, Texas: Word Inc., 1984.

Jones, G. Brian, and Phillips-Jones, Linda. *A Fight to the Better End.* Wheaton, Ill.: Victor Books, 1989.

Leas, Speed, and Kittlaus, Paul. *Church Fights.* Philadelphia: Westminster Press, 1973.

Leas, Speed. *Creative Leadership Series.* Nashville: Abingdon Press, 1982.

McSwain, Larry L., and Treadwell, William C., Jr. *Conflict Ministry in the Church.* Nashville: Broadman Press, 1981.

Schaller, Lyle E. *Activating the Passive Church.* Nashville: Abingdon Press, 1981.

Wiebe, Ronald W., and Rowlison, Bruce A. *Let's Talk about Church Staff Relations.* Alhambra, Calif.: Green Leaf Press, 1983.

MEDITATIONS FOR COMMUNICATION

Finally, brethren, whatever is true, whatever is honorable, whatever is right, whatever is pure, whatever is lovely, whatever is of good repute, if there is any excellence and if anything worthy of praise, let your mind dwell on these things (Philippians 4:8).

Let your speech always be with grace, seasoned, as it were, with salt, so that you may know how you should respond to each person (Colossians 4:6).

But let every one be quick to hear, slow to speak and slow to anger (James 1:19).

A gentle answer turns away wrath, but a harsh word stirs up anger (Proverbs 15:1).

Like apples of gold in settings of silver is a word spoken in right circumstances (Proverbs 25:11).

Chapter 9

Resources for Communication

■ DISCUSSION MODULE 9.1
THE REAL MEANING OF COMMUNICATION

Communication is relationship-building. It involves exchanging information in a way that influences behavior and builds a relationship. Communication is thus much more than merely sending and receiving messages. The information must be sent, received, understood, acted upon, and followed up on. Seen in this light, communication is an active, systematic, interpersonal process that shapes the way people work together.

Rarely is miscommunication so simple as poor word choice or use of the wrong communication channel. Breakdowns in communication usually reflect deeper-seated problems: disagreement about goals and priorities, lack of rapport between team members, conflicting expectations, hidden agendas, and so on. Poor communication is actually more a symptom than a problem. The real problem is dysfunctional relationships within the organization. When relationships break down, so does communication.

Many times *conflicting frames of reference* contribute to shaky relationships in the ministry and hence inferior communication. People are on different "wavelengths" due to differences in age, past experience, technical orientation, and personal needs. This makes it difficult for them to perceive things in the same way, prompting such frustrated comments as, "Those people just don't understand what we're trying to do here," or "They act like their work is more important than ours!"

Selective perception is another common culprit in miscommunication. We all have a tendency to block out information that conflicts with our beliefs and biases—we hear only what we want to hear. For example, if we have an "ax to grind" with a certain program, we may pay exclusive attention to its weak points and shortcomings while conveniently overlooking its virtues.

A third potential communications trap is *source credibility*. The reality that we tend to communicate more effectively with people we trust and respect, highlights the importance of interpersonal rapport in the communication process. It is potentially dangerous for newcomers with little experience to be placed in key positions of communication within the organization. People who don't know them well and haven't established much rapport may not always hear what was actually said or meant.

One additional source of miscommunication is *filtering,* the almost subconscious process of slightly distorting or fudging information to make the sender look good or back the sender's agenda. The ministry leader, for example, might report that team productivity is up twenty percent, yet fail to mention that staff expenses are up fifty percent due to three new persons being hired!

Given the potential for the above four problems, as well as other challenges such as time pressures and role overload, it is not surprising that communication is normally the most imperfect of management functions within Christian organizations. The following Situation Review and Action Plan can help ministry managers weed out needless miscommunication.

▲ SITUATION REVIEW 9.1
THE POTENTIAL FOR MISCOMMUNICATION

Working on an individual basis, ministry team members should state how much they agree with the following statements (2 = strongly agree, 1 = agree, and 0 = disagree).

_____ 1. I know my team members well enough to predict how each will react to what goes on in the ministry.

_____ 2. Team members rarely misunderstand or misinterpret my actions and intentions.

_____ 3. When people disagree with me, it's hard for me to see things from their point of view.

_____ 4. When our team meets, we spend most of our time looking for ways to agree with one another.

_____ 5. My team members have developed high rapport with one another.

_____ 6. Our team tends to think very much alike.

_____ 7. Team conversations are based more on facts and information than on opinions and feelings.

_____ 8. We don't always follow up on the things we talk about at team meetings.

_____ 9. I am often surprised by the actions or statements of my team members.

_____ 10. I have a high degree of trust for my team members.

Score the inventory by subtracting the total for statements 3, 8, and 9 (factors promoting miscommunication) from the total for 1, 2, 4, 5, 6, 7, and 10 (factors preventing miscommunication). Final scores below 5 on the part of many team members (on a ten-point scale), point to less than ideal circumstances for effective communication. Action Plan 9.1 will prove helpful in improving the communications climate.

● ACTION PLAN 9.1
AVOIDING COMMUNICATIONS QUICKSAND

1. The following questions can be used in planning for an important team communication:

Message or purpose of the communication: _____

_____

A. Who is this communication intended to reach?

_____

_____

_____

B. What specific impact do you want this communication to have?
   (How should it influence the behavior of those it is sent to?)

_____

_____

_____

_____

C. How will you know if you have successfully communicated?
   What standard of measure will you use?

_____

_____

_____

_____

_____

D. What follow-up actions can you take to enhance the effectiveness of this communication?

_____

_____

_____

_____

2. Further analyze the communication in Part 1 with these questions:

A. In which of the following areas are you probably on a differ-
ent wavelength from the people you are sending this com-
munication to:
____ Education level
____ Type of technical work performed
____ Job experience
____ Goals and priorities
____ Personal needs
____ Level of influence in the organization

B. Describe how each of the following can help you get on the
same wavelength as the person you are communicating with:
1. Appealing to their personal needs:

_____

_____

_____

2. Dealing with any biases they may (perhaps unknowingly)
have:

_____

_____

_____

3. Furthering their goals:

_____

_____

_____

_____

4. Building trust and rapport:

_____

_____

_____

_____

■ DISCUSSION MODULE 9.2
THE ROLE OF PERCEPTIONS AND
EXPECTATIONS IN COMMUNICATION

Behavior is based in large part on perceptions and expectations—on our subjective view of reality. A key function of communication is to better ground people's perceptions and expectations in organizational reality. False expectations and distorted perceptions can be very damaging to morale and a continuing source of conflict.

Expectations are shaped by two major perceptions: what we perceive the organization wants to do, and what it is capable of doing. Ministry leaders must carefully assess the potential impact of all communications on these two factors. Team unity will fall apart to the extent that members misperceive organization goals and capabilities.

Ministry leaders must be careful not to promise, or even imply, more than they can realistically deliver. They should rely on sound facts and figures in explaining decisions and stay away from "guesstimates" and hunches. Because people have a natural tendency to overreact to what is said and done by those in authority, leaders should carefully avoid the use of hyperbole, oversell, and "pie-in-the-sky" rhetoric.

Some leaders may have to overcome the opposite tendency to be noncommital and vague about events in the organization—"if they can't pin me down, they won't blame me for any failures." Reality orientation is a key leadership responsibility that demands communication finesse and subtlety. Situation Review 9.2 and Action Plan 9.2 will help ministry leaders polish their communication skills.

▲ SITUATION REVIEW 9.2
COMMUNICATION CHECK

Team members should respond to the following questions on an *individual basis:*

1. What are the three most significant things you expect your team to accomplish in the next twelve months?

A. _____

_____

B. _____

_____

C. _____

_____

2. What are your team's three greatest limitations?

A. _____

_____

B. _____

_____

C. _____

_____

3. What two things are most important to your team leader?

A. _____

_____

B. _____

_____

C. _____

_____

4. What does your organization most want your team to accomplish?

_____

_____

_____

5. What role are you expected to play on your team?

_____

_____

_____

6. What two things do you most expect from the other members of your team?

A. _____

_____

B. _____

_____

7. What do you *not* expect your team to accomplish in the next twelve months?

_____

_____

_____

_____

_____

8. How are you perceived by the other members of your team?

_____

_____

_____

_____

_____

9. How is your team leader perceived?

_____

_____

_____

_____

10. How is your particular team or unit perceived by the overall ministry organization?

_____

_____

_____

_____

_____

● **ACTION PLAN 9.2**
GETTING ON THE SAME WAVELENGTH

The responses of individual team members to Situation Review 9.2 should be compared and contrasted in light of the following questions:
1. To what extent do the members of your team seem to have similar

expectations for team performance?

_____

_____

_____

_____

_____

2. Is the team perceived to have many significant limitations? Are these perceptions accurate?

_____

_____

_____

_____

_____

3. Has your team accurately perceived the leader's vision?

_____

_____

_____

_____

_____

4. To what extent does your team appear to be on the same wavelength as the overall organization?

_____

_____

_____

_____

_____

5. Are the members of your team on the same wavelength?

_____

_____

_____

_____

_____

6. In what three primary ways could the team improve its reality-orientation?

A. _____

_____

B. _____

_____

C. _____

_____

■ DISCUSSION MODULE 9.3
COMMUNICATION STYLES

Each of us has a unique communication style to match our unique personality. Not only do we express ourselves in a distinctive way, we perceive the world a bit differently than anyone else, interact with others in a characteristic way, and subscribe to our own goals and priorities.

Some of us are talkers, others are listeners. Some are calm, others emotional. We're not all equally patient, or self-confident, or serious in demeanor. Some of us are idealistic, others practical. We vary in the extent to which we communicate by words, actions, and example. The human communication process indeed reflects diversity.

Coping with the array of styles is the ministry manager's central communications challenge. Team members should be managed in such a way that their communication styles complement one another—one person's communication strengths shore up another's deficiencies. Talkers can be encouraged to listen and listeners encouraged to talk. Forceful team members can be used to help set the record straight, while learning tact from the less blunt but more sensitive members of the group. The optimists can encourage the pessimists, who in turn can temper extreme team excesses.

In short, team communication should be managed so that team members communicate more effectively within the group than they do by themselves. The group should create communications synergy, where deficiencies of individual team members are compensated for and counterbalanced by the larger team. Ideally each person should make a one-of-a-kind contribution to the team's overall communications effectiveness. Without each member's unique communication style the team would suffer.

▲ SITUATION REVIEW 9.3
DESCRIBING YOUR OWN COMMUNICATION STYLE

1. Place an "X" where you feel you fit on each of the scales below dealing with personal communication style.

Talker	Listener
Calm	Emotional
Patient	Impatient
Blunt	Subtle
Easy going	Serious
Spontaneous	Planned
Optimistic	Pessimistic
Encourager	Challenger

Soft	Tough
Abstract	Concrete
Domineering	Compliant
Subjective	Objective
Opinionated	Factual
Cautious	Decisive

2. Have team members indicate (in different colored ink) what they feel is your own communications style on each of the continuums in the section above.

● ACTION PLAN 9.3
INCREASING COMMUNICATION SYNERGY

Individual team members should use the following questions in assessing the results of Situation Review 9.3.

1. To what extent have you and your team agreed in the assessment of your personal communications style?

_____

_____

_____

2. What are your communication tendencies?

_____

_____

_____

_____

_____

3. Which of these communication tendencies make positive contributions to the success of your individual ministry? Why does this occur?

_____

_____

_____

_____

_____

_____

4. Which of your communication tendencies limit your ministry success? Why?

_____

_____

_____

_____

_____

5. Identify three specific actions that will enhance your ability to communicate effectively:

A. _____

_____

B. _____

_____

C. _____

_____

6. What can you do to help other members of your team communicate more effectively?

_____

_____

_____

_____

_____

■ DISCUSSION MODULE 9.4
SITUATIONAL COMMUNICATION

The form of communication—verbal, written, group, one-on-one, formal, informal—must match the situation at hand. With so many forms of communication available, it is not always easy to choose the most appropriate approach. Yet "synchronized" communication, involving a good fit between channel and situation, is essential for on-going ministry success.

In planning a message, the ministry manager has three general communication categories to consider. Should the communication be _personal_ or _impersonal; formal_ or _informal; written_ or _verbal?_ Different communication situations call for different combinations of these categories.

Communication should be personalized, involving direct contact between sender and receiver, whenever people's feelings are involved as much as their thoughts. Strictly informational communication, such as ministry current event updates or calendar prompts, don't normally require person-to-person contact because people's feelings aren't involved. However, when the communication is not of a routine informational nature and will evoke a reaction from the receiver, personalized contact of some form is essential.

Official communications, involving matters of policy and precedent, should be made through formal channels such as agenda-backed meetings or documentation in a manual. By contrast, most day-to-day communications to coordinate work should be approached informally via hallway conversations, impromptu planning sessions, and telephone chats. Informal communication is usually the most efficient and convenient way to coordinate daily work agendas. More formal approaches, such as managing by memo or frequently called committee meetings only tend to create a burgeoning bureaucracy.

Again, deciding whether to communicate verbally or in writing depends on the situation. Lengthy and technical messages requiring little feedback—detailed instructions, reports, policies and procedures—should be written to permit close scrutiny and repeated referrals. Verbal channels should be used whenever exchange and feedback are important: delegating work assignments, coordinating workflow, troubleshooting problems, analyzing decision-making alternatives, and so forth.

Situation Review 9.4 and Action Plan 9.4 offer guidance for matching the form of communication to the situation.

▲ SITUATION REVIEW 9.4
MIXING AND MATCHING COMMUNICATION

1. Throughout a typical work week, team members should keep track of the types of communication they engage in and the communication channels employed. The summary chart below can be filled out as the week progresses. Each time a team member engages in one of the forms, or channels of communication, he or she should use the space provided to write down the letter of the purpose of the communication as outlined below.

Weekly Communication Log
Communication Channels

Personal: _____

_____

Impersonal: _____

_____

Formal: _____

_____

Informal: _____

_____

Written: _____

Verbal: _____

Purpose of the Communication
A. Giving work instructions for a specific short-term task.
B. Explaining a major policy or procedure.
C. Enforcing a policy, procedure, or rule.
D. Praising or critiquing a team member's performance.
E. Implementing change.
F. Resolving conflict.
G. Putting out minor brushfires.
H. Analyzing courses of action for a decision.
I. Updating the team about current organizational events.
J. Planning major assignments or projects.
K. Initiating change.

2. The completed weekly communication log should be analyzed by totaling up the letters recorded within each of the six broad communication channels. These totals can be entered in the following spaces:

	A	B	C	D	E	F	G	H	I	J	K
Personal											
Impersonal											
Formal											
Informal											
Written											
Verbal											
Column Totals:											

The following chart matches up the eleven types of communication (A-K) with the channels that are usually most effective and situationally appropriate.

> ## Effective Communication Match-Ups

Personal: A-C-D-E-F-G-H-J-K
Impersonal: B-H-I
Formal: B-E-I-J-K
Informal: A-C-D-E-F-G-H-K
Written: B-E-H-I-J
Verbal: A-B-C-D-E-F-G-H-J-K

The above match-up chart clearly indicates that, as a general rule, some communication channels (personal, informal, and verbal) should be used more frequently in Christian organizations than other channels (impersonal, formal, and written).

3. Analyze the apparent situational effectiveness of your own communication style by answering the following questions:

A. Which communication channels do you tend to use most frequently?

_____

B. How does your response to question 1 compare with the Effective Communication Match-Ups chart?

_____

_____

_____

C. According to your assessment, do you tend to overuse some communications channels and underutilize others?

_____

_____

_____

D. Does your communication style tend to be overly formal or overly informal? Would you characterize it as fairly well-balanced situationally?

_____

_____

_____

E. In which situation do you have a tendency to use an inappropriate channel of communication?

_____

_____

_____

● ACTION PLAN 9.4
FINE-TUNING YOUR COMMUNICATION STYLE

1. Which channels of communication do you want to use more frequently to improve your situational effectiveness?

_____

_____

_____

2. Which channels do you want to rely on less?

_____

_____

_____

3. Explain how you could make more effective use of the *six* communication channels:

Personal: _____

_____

_____

Impersonal: _____

_____

_____

Formal: _____

_____

_____

Informal: _____

_____

_____

Written: _____

_____

_____

Verbal: _____

_____

_____

■ DISCUSSION MODULE 9.5
BUILDING RELATIONSHIPS
THROUGH COMMUNICATION

The ultimate purpose of communication is relationship-building (not mere message-sending), and the key to relationships is interpersonal rapport. We build rapport by showing concern not only for the professional side of our team members (what they produce and how they perform), but also for their personal side (e.g., their individuality, interests, family). Rapport involves having a growing relationship with the whole person, not just part of the person.

Relationships of this depth rarely develop automatically—they must be patiently nurtured through creative communication. Four communication skills are the nucleus of rapport: listening, tact, positive reinforcement, and loving confrontation.

Listening is the single most useful tool in any manager's arsenal, because it "speaks" volumes about your interest in the other person and insures that the crucial feedback loop in communication is completed. Naive communicators too quickly assume that talking is power; in reality listening is, because of its rapport-building potential. Indeed it is true that "one pair of listening ears can drink a thousand tongues dry." People who say they don't have the time to listen are really expressing their unwillingness to build relationships!

Rapport is also advanced through *tactfulness*, the capacity for communicating negative messages in a positive, constructive manner. Tactfulness does not mean telling people only what they want to hear or ingenuously "sugar-coating" communications, but it does entail phrasing unflattering or unwelcome messages in a face-saving, ego-protecting manner. Tact signals that you care enough about the other person to use words that affirm their humanity.

Proverbs eloquently states the communication principles of *positive reinforcement:* "How delightful is a timely word" (15:23) and "Anxiety in the heart of a man weighs it down, but a good word makes it glad" (12:25). The potential of positive reinforcement goes well beyond praise to include any form of accepting a particular action or behavior: references to contributions made, public recognition, even imitation of the same behavior. When we positively reinforce a team member, we communicate our acceptance and approval. Rapport is inevitable!

Rapport also has a tough side. It takes courage to confront someone in love as a means of improving your relationship. *Loving confrontation* says I care about you too much to allow our relationship to stagnate or deteriorate.

The Situation Review and Action Plan that follow provide practical guidelines for communicating your way into better relationships.

▲ SITUATION REVIEW 9.5
RAPPORT REPORT

Team members should indicate how much they agree with the following statements (2 = strongly agree, 1 = agree, and 0 = disagree).
_____ 1. I tend to be all business in my relationships with team members.

_____ 2. I don't hesitate to reveal my "inner self" when working with others.

_____ 3. In most situations, I'm too impatient to be a good listener.

_____ 4. Even when I'm busy, I make time to praise the efforts of fellow workers.

_____ 5. When I have a relationship problem, I usually wait for the other person to take the first step in resolving it.

_____ 6. I try to keep in close touch with the work activities of my team members.

_____ 7. I am quicker to point out someone's faults and shortcomings than their strengths.

_____ 8. I learn a great deal about the needs of this ministry by regularly listening to others.

_____ 9. I am usually more concerned with what I want to say than with how I will say it.

_____ 10. People are generally very willing to listen to me.

Score the inventory by subtracting the total for the odd-numbered statements (factors damaging rapport) from the total for the even-numbered ones (factors supporting rapport). The higher your final score on a 10-point scale, the greater your rapport-building effectiveness appears to be. People with relatively low scores should put forth a more systematic effort to build rapport. Action Plan 9.5 provides help.

● ACTION PLAN 9.5
RAPPORT PLANNING

1. Place a check beside each rapport-builder below that is not an established part of your communication style. Consult your responses to Situation Review 9.5 as a guide.

_____ Getting to know team members as people, not just as professionals.

_____ Revealing your human side to others.

_____ Listening patiently and receptively.

_____ Praising others when they deserve it.

_____ Taking the initiative in building relationships with others.

_____ Staying in close touch with the daily work activities of team members.

_____ Accentuating the positive rather than the negative about others.

_____ Learning through listening.

_____ Tactfulness and diplomacy.

_____ Loving confrontation.

2. In the provided space, list your excuses for not using each rapport-builder to the maximum:

Listening: _____

_____

_____

Taking the initiative in relationship-building: _____

_____

_____

Positively reinforcing others: _____

_____

_____

Tactfulness: _____

_____

_____

Loving confrontation: _____

_____

_____

Now crumple up this list, throw it away, and resolve to never again rely on these excuses!

RESOURCES ON COMMUNICATION

Buchanan, Edward A. *Developing Leadership Skills.* Nashville: Convention Press, 1971.

Eims, Leroy. *Be A Motivational Leader.* Wheaton, Ill.: Victor Books, 1982.

Engstrom, Ted W. *Your Gift Of Administration.* Nashville: Thomas Nelson Publishers, 1982.

Engstrom, Ted W.; Dayton, Edward R. *60-Second Management Guide.* Waco, Texas: Word Inc., 1984.

Haggai, John. *Lead On!* Waco, Texas: Word Inc., 1986.

Rush, Myron, *Management: A Biblical Approach.* Wheaton, Ill.: Victor Books, 1983.

Sanders, J. Oswald. *Paul the Leader.* Colorado Springs: Navpress, 1984.

MEDITATIONS FOR STAFFING AND PROFESSIONAL DEVELOPMENT

I know how to get along with humble means, and I also know how to live in prosperity; in any and every circumstance I have learned the secret of being filled and going hungry, both of having abundance and suffering need. I can do all things through Him who strengthens me (Philippians 4:12-13).

As you therefore have received Christ Jesus the Lord, so walk in Him, having been firmly rooted and now being built up in Him and established in your faith, just as you were instructed, and overflowing with gratitude (Colossians 2:6-7).

Whatever you do, do your work heartily, as for the Lord rather than for men (Colossians 3:23).

Be diligent to present yourself approved to God as a workman who does not need to be ashamed, handling accurately the word of truth (2 Timothy 2:15).

Like a city that is broken into and without walls is a man who has no control over his spirit (Proverbs 25:28).

Chapter 10

Resources for Staffing and Professional Development

■ DISCUSSION MODULE 10.1
CATALYSTS TO PERSONAL PRODUCTIVITY
IN CHRISTIAN ORGANIZATIONS

Although the ingredients of *personal productivity* are numerous and diverse, a more limited set of factors serve as catalysts to performance. These catalysts, which are both personal and interpersonal in origin, stimulate individual performance and facilitate teamwork. Three such catalysts are of particular importance to Christian professionals: organization culture, job descriptions, and creative stress.

Just as people have unique personalities, each ministry has an *organization culture* all its own. This culture revolves around what the group values, how people do their work and make decisions, and how the organization relates to the outside world. Culture is a direct reflection of the organization's membership, and particularly its leaders.

Some personalities and temperaments blend into the culture better than others, making organizational compatibility crucially important. The organization must hire people who are not only technically competent, but who also fit into the established internal culture. Organizational fit is just as much a catalyst for productivity as job competence. This is especially true for ministries, which rely so heavily on the right "chemistry" between idealistic staff and volunteers. "Fitting in" becomes just as important for success as training and experience.

Job descriptions can be a second powerful catalyst for productivity. When managed effectively, the job description telegraphs performance expectations and creates a sense of urgency about working. Unfortunately, too many bureaucracy-addicted organizations misuse job descriptions to merely passively describe job duties and procedures.

Well written job descriptions highlight the organizational contributions each job is expected to make—how the job will benefit others and advance the organization's mission. "Job contributions" would actually be a better name for job descriptions, as well as a more accurate reflection of how they boost productivity. When people focus on contributions, they are generally much more productive and fulfilled than when they focus on "standard operating procedure."

A potent, but seldom recognized, performance catalyst can be called *creative stress*—using natural job-related stress as the basis for continuing professional development. The concept of creative stress recognizes the dynamic potential of pain to drive performance. The cliche, "no pain—no gain," reflects an important truth. Until we are stretched and challenged in our work, we can't fully realize our potential.

The constructive side of stress has long been recognized, but rarely actively managed. Tolerable amounts of stress nudge us out of our lethargy and prick our productive potential. Pressuring someone to produce is not always bad when done to tap latent creativity and ability. Used creatively, small doses of stress can break the logjam of self-imposed routine of "business-as-usual."

Situation Review 10.1 and Action Plan 10.1 provide concrete guidelines for managing these three performance catalysts.

▲ SITUATION REVIEW 10.1
CATALYSTS OR LOGJAMS?

1. Ministry team members should check either response 1 or 2 for each statement below:
   A. Our ministry hires or recruits new members mainly on the basis of:
   _____ 1. Their technical competence.
   _____ 2. Their personality and temperament.
   B. To the extent that our ministry uses job descriptions (either formally in writing or informally through word of mouth), we emphasize:

_____ 1. The duties and procedures of the job.

_____ 2. The contributions and outputs (results) of the job.

C. Job stress tends to:

_____ 1. Drain the members of this ministry.

_____ 2. Stimulate them to strive for higher achievement.

D. I generally view job stress as something to be:

_____ 1. Avoided.

_____ 2. Creatively managed.

E. Job descriptions within our ministry tend to be:

_____ 1. Ignored or taken for granted.

_____ 2. Used as a challenge to spur performance.

F. The culture of this organization stresses:

_____ 1. Busyness.

_____ 2. Accomplishment.

G. _____ 1. We never give much thought to the culture of our organization.

_____ 2. We are aware of our organizational culture and try to work in ways compatible to it.

The more "2" responses checked the better, because they reflect progressive approaches to professional development. Action Plan 10.1 goes a step further by providing planning guidelines for progressive professional development.

2. From the list below, place a plus (+) sign beside the five items that best describe the culture of your ministry or organization. Place a minus (-) sign beside the five items that least describe your culture. This exercise should be completed by _the entire team_ as a group.

_____ Fast changing

_____ Stable

_____ Entrepreneurial (constantly seeking new opportunities)

_____ Traditional (preserving the status quo)

_____ Performance-focused

_____ Relationships-focused

_____ Creative

_____ Formal and organized

_____ Informal and spontaneous

_____ Competitive

_____ Cooperative

_____ Authoritarian (power held by few people)

_____ Decentralized (power widely dispersed)

_____ Insulated (limited interaction with people not on the ministry team)

_____ Networked (extensive interaction with people outside the ministry team)

_____ Paternalistic (high tolerance of team member shortcomings and failures)

_____ Demanding (everyone is expected to do their job)

_____ Future-focused

_____ Present-focused

_____ Short-run emphasis

_____ Long-run emphasis

_____ Personal

_____ Impersonal

_____ Making things happen

_____ Waiting for things to happen

_____ High consensus

_____ High conflict

_____ (Other):

_____ (Other):

● ACTION PLAN 10.1
CREATING A CLIMATE FOR PROGRESSIVE PROFESSIONAL DEVELOPMENT

1. Based on your organization culture portrait in part 2 of Situation Review 10.1, list six personal characteristics of the type of person who will readily fit in with your ministry team:

A.

B.

C.

D.

E.

F.

2. Characterize people who would probably not fit in with the team as easily:

A. _____

_____

B. _____

_____

C. _____

_____

D. _____

_____

E. _____

_____

3. Every worker should review his or her job. Each team member should then list the primary contributions he or she makes to the overall ministry team:

_____

_____

_____

_____

_____

4. Phrase each of the ministry contributions mentioned in question 3 as a specific job goal:

_____

_____

_____

_____

_____

5. What causes you the greatest amount of job stress?

_____

_____

_____

_____

_____

6. State three ways in which these stressors can potentially contribute to your professional development:

A. _____

_____

B. _____

_____

C. _____

_____

■ DISCUSSION MODULE 10.2
CATALYSTS TO TEAM PRODUCTIVITY

Organization culture, job descriptions, and creative stress can serve as catalysts to personal productivity, which is the first phase of professional development. The second phase is *team productivity,* in which team members develop skills and capabilities that transcend individual performance and enhance the overall team's capacity to perform. In this vital second phase of professional development, individual productivity becomes the catalyst for team performance. Three basic processes are involved: mentoring, networking, and innovation.

Team members who have the strongest people orientation possess the greatest potential to serve as *mentors*—people who systematically build themselves into other people. Mentors form a bridge between the team and its individual members, thereby bonding the part with the whole. Mentors act as a communication conduit between the organization and its members, sharing the vision and facilitating synergistic teamwork. Mentors place productive relationship-building ahead of individual productivity and competitiveness. Team members who have largely mastered their own productivity and want to exert a greater impact on others are ideal candidates for mentoring. They are leaders who want to help others become better followers.

Team productivity is further fueled by *networking*, the interactive, interpersonal process of building alliances outside the team with important individuals and groups. Every member of the team can and should have a role in building the team's network, which is the sum total of all external team member contacts.

Networking enhances professional development because outsiders are the primary source of reality orientation for team members. As team members interact with outsiders, they gain invaluable insight into the team itself. The network tells the team how well it is performing and where and when change is needed. It serves as a mirror that reflects reality.

Innovation is the third and most telling phase of team productivity. Has the professional development of team members progressed to the point where they can consistently rise above the ministry's prevailing status quo and create something better?

Innovative team members create new opportunities for service and additional ways to serve. They expand the ministry's vision and provide fresh perspective. Sometimes they may even reinvent the ministry and help fellow team members internalize the new vision.

Innovation creates new solutions to old problems and redefines problems so that old solutions work once again. It sees victory in defeat, opportunity in conflict, and a new start in every ending. Above all, innovation convincingly shows team members that they can make a noticeable difference in the ministry.

▲ SITUATION REVIEW 10.2
TRANSCENDING THE INDIVIDUAL

Working individually, team members should indicate how strongly they agree with each statement below (2 = strongly agree, 1 = agree, and 0 = disagree).

___ 1. I would like to have a greater impact on my team.
___ 2. Team accomplishments are more important than my own individual contributions.
___ 3. I have largely mastered my job on the team.
___ 4. I have keen insight into what makes the team successful.
___ 5. Even when I'm busy, I make time for others during the work day.
___ 6. I enjoy meeting people and making new contacts.
___ 7. Talking with others usually gives me a lot of ideas.
___ 8. I'm a fairly change-oriented person.
___ 9. I think about my team and its mission quite often.
___ 10. I have a vision for my work and for the team's work.

Add up your ten responses and derive an overall total. All the statements represent positive catalysts to team productivity. The closer your score is to 20, the greater your potential for functioning as a team catalyst.

● ACTION PLAN 10.2
TEAM CATALYST PRIORITIES

Rank the following ten team contributions in order of their potential for you. Rank as number 1 the item that promises to be your largest new team contribution; rank the second largest as number 2, and so on through 10.

___ Keeping in closer touch with the work and contributions of each team member.
___ Spending more time with individual team members one-on-one.
___ Spending more time with the team as an overall group.
___ Challenging team members to higher standards of performance.
___ Encouraging and praising team members more consistently.
___ Engaging in external networking for the team (meeting new people, getting to know outsiders better, etc.).
___ Doing mundane work for the team to free up members to serve in other capacities.
___ Stimulating creative new ideas.
___ Helping to champion and implement new ideas.
___ Recruiting new members to join the team.

■ DISCUSSION MODULE 10.3
PERFORMANCE EVALUATION

In most organizations, performance evaluation is an unlikely candidate for the manager's most popular job duty. Managers, as well as team members, typically dread performance evaluation because they perceive a strong potential for conflict, embarrassment, and wasted time. Indeed in many organizations this may be the dismal legacy of performance evaluation, but only when it is mishandled and misunderstood. When approached in the right way, performance evaluation should be an enjoyable, positive process that benefits everyone.

The problem with performance evaluation is reflected in the very name itself—evaluating performance. *Actually it is not performance that should be evaluated, but contributions.* Placing the emphasis on performance implies a philosophy of management that should be alien to Christian organizations: valuing people for what they do rather than for who they are in Christ. The distinction is more than semantics.

When people get the impression, whether conscious or subconscious, that they are not accepted unconditionally by their organization, a host of tensions and frustrations can develop that often reach crisis proportions at the annual evaluation. "Will I keep my job?" "What do they think of me this year?" "What more can they possibly ask of me?" "I wonder who will be in the dog house next?"

The problem with performance evaluation in most organizations is that people feel they, not their performance, are really being evaluated. No wonder the entire undertaking is so often surrounded with anxiety! It need not be so. By emphasizing contributions rather than performance, the process takes on a different, more appealing, aura. The concept of "contributions analysis" does more than sound positive compared to performance evaluation. It makes most people feel positive because of the implication of service rendered.

People feel good about serving and appreciate occasions when the organization recognizes their contributions and provides additional opportunities to serve. Even though we don't all make the same number of contributions, we do all enjoy serving. Performance evaluation should be part of the enjoyment.

But what about team members who have lagged in their service contributions? How can something positive come out of performance evaluation for them? Again, efforts must be made to accentuate the positive by pointing out opportunities for greater service. This should not be seen as a condition for accepting the team member, but rather as an avenue for greater self-fulfillment.

Even when it is necessary to take drastic action over unsatisfactory team member performance—such as retraining, reassignment, or even termination—emphasis must be placed on affirming that person's inherent worth apart from his or her performance in a given team role. Difficult staffing decisions must be made from time to time in every organization, including idealistic Christian ones, but they can be done in a way that affirms and upholds the individual.

Situation Review 10.3 and Action Plan 10.3 provide a framework for conducting performance evaluation in a positive, affirming way.

▲ SITUATION REVIEW 10.3
ME OR MY PERFORMANCE?

Individual team members should indicate how strongly they agree with each of the following statements (2 = strongly agree, 1 = agree, and 0 = disagree).

_____ 1. My team appreciates me as a person regardless of how I perform.

_____ 2. I enjoy my job even when I don't get the recognition I deserve.

_____ 3. My team helps me see the benefits of my performance.

_____ 4. My job fits into the larger vision of this organization.

_____ 5. I appreciate advice that helps me to be of greater service to the ministry.

_____ 6. I'm more concerned with what's best for the ministry than with what's best for me.

_____ 7. I'm comfortable with the fact that my co-workers don't all have the same responsibilities or make the same contributions.

The seven statements (representing positive attitudes) should be totaled, yielding a maximum score of 14. High scores reflect a positive attitude about performance with an emphasis on team member uniqueness and contributions. Low scores on the part of many team members may indicate they are accepted only if they meet the performance expectations of others.

● ACTION PLAN 10.3
AFFIRMATIVE PERFORMANCE EVALUATION

Use the following questions as a framework for evaluating team member performance in an affirming way.

1. Who benefited by the way you performed your job?

_____

_____

_____

2. How did the people listed in question 1 benefit?

_____

_____

_____

_____

_____

3. In what additional ways do you wish people would have benefited from your performance?

_____

_____

_____

_____

_____

4. What unexpected benefits came from your job performance?

_____

_____

_____

_____

5. How do the members of your team perceive your job performance?

_____

_____

_____

6. How can team members help you further increase your job contributions?

_____

_____

_____

_____

7. How can you help team members increase their contributions?

_____

_____

_____

_____

RESOURCES ON STAFFING
AND PROFESSIONAL DEVELOPMENT

Engstrom, Ted W., and Dayton, Edward R. *60-Second Management Guide.* Waco, Texas: Word Inc., 1984.

Johnson, Douglas W. *Creative Leadership Series.* Nashville: Abingdon Press, 1982.

Knudson, Raymond B. *New Models For Church Administration.* Chicago: Follett Publishing, 1979.

Powers, Bruce P. *Church Administration Handbook.* Nashville: Broadman Press, 1985.

Schaller, Lyle E. *The Multiple Staff and the Larger Church.* Nashville: Abingdon Press, 1980.

Wiebe, Ronald W.; Rowlison, Bruce A. *Let's Talk About Church Staff Relationships.* Alhambra, Calif.: Green Leaf Press, 1983.

EPILOGUE

A CONCLUDING PERSPECTIVE:
TEAMWORK WITH A DIFFERENCE; TEAMWORK
THAT MAKES A DIFFERENCE

Christian ministry is teamwork with a difference, teamwork that makes a difference. This is because Christians are different in the goals they pursue and in the way they pursue them. God intends for His family members to work together in unified cooperation, the very essence of teamwork.

Christian ministry is teamwork with a difference because of the pervasive sense of family. Members of the team are valued not only for their work contributions but also for who they are as members of Christ's body—their spiritual equality enables them to relate to one another in an authentic, loving manner.

Christian ministry is teamwork with a difference because personal sacrifice is elevated above rugged individualism and self-serving competitiveness. Team members thrive on serving others and in putting their needs first. Mutual sacrifice becomes a way of life as team members willingly give of themselves for the good of the ministry and the people it serves.

Christian ministry is teamwork with a difference because followers are just as important as leaders. God uses the efforts of each team member in equally important ways, all unique and special. A collective vision is shared, born of the team members' collective wisdom, submission, and accountability. "We" triumphs over "me."

Above all, Christian ministry is teamwork with a difference because God is in the driver's seat. *He* charts the ultimate course. Only through the team's keen sense of obedience and dependence can the ministry ever succeed. Christian teamwork is God-focused.

Christian ministry is also teamwork that makes a difference—a difference in what is produced and in how people feel about their work. Christians are called to be hard workers, optimistic workers, and fruitful workers. They are to labor because they want to, not because they have to. They are to work together cooperatively, enthusiastically, and positively. When they faithfully do these things, it makes a big difference in what the team is able to accomplish—in what God is able to accomplish.

The perspective of Christian ministry developed in this book is founded on six foundational principles of teamwork. The leader who recognizes and follows these principles will be able to generate team-work that truly makes a difference.

1. *The niche principle:* People who occupy a special place on the team feel special and perform in a special way. Team niches humanize teamwork.

2. *The ownership principle:* The more team members participate in running the team (decision-making, planning, coordinating, and so on), the more they will own the team's goals and mission. Ownership breeds personal and interpersonal accountability.

3. *The trust principle:* People who share a common vision, who personalize the work process, and who accept one another in *agape* love come to trust one another. Trust is the glue that binds the team together through thick and thin.

4. *The interaction principle:* The more people interact, the more they bond. Bonded people share with one another and bear with one another.

5. *The submission principle:* People who submit to one another elevate the team above the individual. This puts the ministry's vision in the forefront, where it can capture the team's attention and energy.

6. *The spirituality principle:* Teams engaged in Christian ministry are supernaturally empowered, generating a rare kind of fruitfulness nurtured by team member unity, vision, and sacrifice. God lovingly shepherds His teams, helping them succeed despite human fallibility and frailty.

Spirituality is the true essence of Christian teamwork—people working together for God and with God. The wise team leader will take this divine partnership seriously, giving prominent attention to team prayer, devotionals, and fellowship. Team members who grow spiritually together will surely grow professionally together. This is teamwork with a difference, teamwork that makes a difference! "But seek first His kingdom and His righteousness; and all these things shall be added to you" (Matt. 6:33).

DATE DUE

DE 20'91			
AP 19'93			
DE 27'93			
12/14/94			
DE 28'04			